PINOT PILOT

The story of Brice Cutrer Jones
and The Great American Pinot Noir

Unabridged Edition

A MEMOIR
BY
BRICE CUTRER JONES

AS TOLD TO
John Brusky

Dedication

They taught me how to fly, pointed me down life's runway,
and launched me into the Wild Blue Yonder,
the wind in my face and a new challenge waiting
behind each cloud.

For all I have done and all I have hoped to do,
for whatever I am and whatever I may have
accomplished, I gratefully dedicate
this book to my parents,
Eleanor and Bill Jones.

Acknowledgments

This book would have never happened if Brusk hadn't prodded me. I think he wanted to finally have the upper hand when dealing with his former roommate and sometimes tormenter.

If you don't like the book, blame Brusk. But if you enjoy it, give all credit to his son, Jimmy, who was responsible for keeping two old aviators on course. Without his superb editing and technical skills, we'd have landed on the wrong runway.

Foreword

In 2019, I finished writing *Pinot Pilot,* the story of my evolution from Air Force pilot to producer of Emeritus Vineyards Pinot Noir, a world-class Burgundy born and raised right here in Sonoma County, California.

Mission accomplished, or so I thought.

But there's always more to tell. And hiding under a rock is just not my style.

So here it is, unvarnished and transparent: *Pinot Pilot, Unabridged Edition*, the story of my life before, during, and after the first *Pinot Pilot* book.

– Brice Jones

Table of Contents

Table of Contents

Chapter		Page

Table of Contents

It's all connected.
Everything.
So put on your g-suit and helmet.
Climb on board. Strap yourself in.
And prepare for takeoff.

-Brice Cutrer Jones

CHAPTER ONE

Eating Kites

I t's 1968, two years after Big George told me that Burgundy is a place and not just the name of a wine. I'm flying F-100s out of Myrtle Beach, South Carolina. Still in the Air Force, but dipping my toe in wine, I'm trying to get a jump start on civilian life. I have a potential land deal with three investors I've never met. Thirty acres out on the high desert near Barstow, California. I want to plant Palomino grapes there and make sherry. Sherry! Oh, Lord.

My friend Joe Higgs, an extraordinarily skilled F-4 fighter pilot, is stationed at George Air Force Base near my prospective sherry vineyard. I want to bring him in on the deal, so we set a date to check out the land. I touch down at George at 2300 hours on a Friday.

Joe meets me in his '57 cherry-red Thunderbird at the ladder of my USAF Super Sabre single-seat jet fighter. Off we go to Joe's apartment where two lovely blondes and a six-pack await.

Next morning, we leave the apartment and the girls and head out to the high desert. Joe has found a prospective winemaker. After an hour or so, we see an oasis ahead. The desert's so flat and the air so clear, we can see it coming ten miles away. No camels at the oasis, just palm trees, a rickety house, and a few vehicles in various states of disrepair. A weathered old guy meets us in front of the house. We get out of Joe's car, and I ask, "You know how to make wine?"

He says, "I know how to grow them wine bushes, sonny."

"You're hired."

We get back in the car and go look at the land. It looks okay to me, but what do I know about land, grapes, or sherry?

Back to Joe's apartment we go. We party the rest of the day and night. Sunday morning, I grab my gear. Gotta get back to Myrtle Beach.

Out at my plane, Joe says, "Hey, give us an airshow when you leave."

An airshow just means a low flyby. Some guys do it upside down or do a roll or some other aerobatic maneuver. The basic flyby is just a low altitude pass. But low means really low. So I agree and strap into the airplane. Joe goes back to his apartment, where he and the girls wait for my airshow.

I taxi out to the runway, but there's a 50-knot wind with a 35-knot crosswind component. I wait for it to die down so I can take off between gusts. Sitting there waiting, engine running, burning gas, I radio the command post and ask them to call a phone number for me and tell whoever answers that I'm gonna be ten minutes late. Finally, I get off between the gusts, level off about 20,000 feet, and call Las Vegas center.

"Vegas, I'll be in the local area for about 15 minutes." I descend to six feet.

I mean low.

Screaming up Apple Valley at about 400 knots, 450 maybe, throwing a rooster tail behind me, blowing over TV antennas, eating kites, I get Joe's apartment complex on my windscreen and go in so low I suck the water right out of the swimming pool. I light the afterburner. I'm gonna shake Joe and the blondes right out of their shoes.

The afterburner is an injection of fuel right into the exhaust, jet fuel sent into the flame. It's like adding a rocket to a jet engine. Gives you a big kick. You throw the throttle outboard to light it, and the tail end of the jet opens wide for the added exhaust. But there can be up to a two-second delay before it lights and the thrust kicks in.

Well, I'm maybe ten feet over the swimming pool, and I throw the throttle outboard. The burner doesn't ignite immediately and while I'm waiting the two seconds for it to light, I've got zero thrust. I have plenty of airspeed, over 400 knots, so I'm not gonna crash. I just start rotating (pulling the nose up). Before the burner kicks in, I go about a quarter mile. I have about a 20-degree angle of attack (nose up) when the afterburner lights. By then I'm over a real estate office, a little shack, basically.

There's a woman inside, maybe closing a sale, smiling, I imagine, saying, "You'll love the peace and quiet of Apple Valley." Then my afterburner lights. Did I mention how loud that is when it ignites? Think of the loudest thunderclap you ever heard, tripled.

Thus shaking up that little shack in peaceful Apple Valley. She loses the sale. She calls the base. But it's Sunday morning. The only people you can get on Sunday morning are in the command post.

"Oh, yes, ma'am. Yes, ma'am. We'll take care of this. There's only one airplane up today, so we know exactly who it is. We'll take care of it. Don't worry. That pilot is toast." The command post guy hangs up, picks up another phone and calls his wing commander.

"Sir, we got this complaint from Apple Valley. A pilot beat up a real estate office. He couldn't have been more than 15 feet high, and this woman lost a sale. She's very upset."

The wing commander says, "Hang him."

"Yes, sir," says the command post guy, Major JB Stone. I never met or heard of him, but he's a fighter pilot, a guy who flies with Joe and the rest of the fighter jocks at George. He's doing his Sunday morning duty in the command post. He's the guy who took my radio call when I said, "Please call this number."

Well, the way this story should play out is he picks up the other phone, calls Myrtle Beach, gets the wing commander, and says, "Your pilot, Captain Brice C. Jones, flying an F-100 from your base, beat up a real estate office, and the woman lost a sale and she's screaming bloody murder and blah, blah and blah." Then when I landed at Myrtle Beach, fat, dumb, and happy, I would've been met by the air police and probably cuffed. I would've been visiting the slammer for a day or two. I would've met an FEB (Flight Evaluation Board) where my wings, my rank, and my future would have been in serious jeopardy.

That's the way it would have gone 99 times out of 100, except that JB Stone is a fighter pilot, not a real command post jockey, who has been ordered by his wing commander to hang me.

"Yes sir. I will." JB Stone sits there and he thinks and he thinks. Finally, he fishes around on his desk and finds the scrap of paper that he wrote the phone number down on when I called and said, "Call this number." He finds that number, dials it.

"Who's this?" JB asks.

"This is Joe Higgs."

"Joe, this is JB out at the command post. Did you have an airshow out there this morning?"

"Oh my God, JB, did we have an airshow? Oh geez, you should've seen him. He sucked all the water out of the pool. He was six feet over the thing, blah, blah, blah."

"Joe. Hey, Joe, calm down. This guy beat up a real estate office about a quarter mile from there, and the woman lost a sale. She's pissed off, so I called the wing commander, and the wing commander told me to hang him."

And Joe Higgs says,

"You can't hang Brice Jones."

JB sits there. Time stands still. Finally, he picks up his phone, calls his wing commander. "Sir, I've been checking around Apple Valley, and there's absolutely nobody out there who corroborates that story. That woman has called before. She's a chronic complainer."

"In that case, forget it."

"Yes sir."

Well, I never did put that sherry deal together, and it's just as well. If I had, I might never have found my way to Burgundy.

CHAPTER TWO

The Toothbrush

My father grew up on a farm in Perry, Oklahoma. When he was six, his mother, Bertie Crawford Jones (my grandmother), died in childbirth. The baby lived less than an hour, but Bertie lived for another day. While she was on her deathbed, she made her sister, Pearl Crawford, a schoolteacher, promise to take care of her children. We can assume Aunt Pearl wasn't too happy when she took over, because she treated Dad and his three siblings, Freeman, Johanna, and Lillian, with coldness and scorn.

Here is a story Dad used to tell my sisters and me at Christmas time:

It was 1916. My mother, your grandmother, had just died. As was the custom at that time in the "Wild West," our aunt moved in and married my father. Then Dad went off to fight the Kaiser. My brother and sisters and I were left with this mean woman who didn't even pretend she liked us. Especially me. I was six years old and felt deserted and heartbroken.

Perry, Oklahoma had sent a lot of her sons to soldier in France, so there were plenty of families without men. Somebody came up with the idea it would be nice for the kids if there was a communal Christmas tree for the families. They cut down a tree and set it up just a short walk from our house. When you're six years old, there's magic in a Christmas tree. Especially when every day new gifts would appear, hanging by colored ribbons from the branches. I used to stand there in awe, fascinated by the tree and the ribboned gifts. When a little toy soldier appeared, nestled in the branches, I felt a thrill of anticipation. "Soon I will be playing with him," I thought. Then one morning, a toothbrush appeared on a branch, hanging there, humble, drab, and out of place. I thought, "Gee whiz, I wonder what unlucky person is getting that."

Christmas morning arrived, and our new "mom" trooped us down to the tree. There were other families gathered round, and—Surprise!—Santa Claus appeared. He sure looked like our postman, but miracles do happen on Christmas morning. But then the second-most-dreadful thing in the world happened. Santa pulled the shiny soldier from the branches and handed it to a kid I liked. Then the absolutely-most-dreadful thing happened. I watched in horror as Santa picked up that toothbrush and dangled it in slow motion as he turned towards me.

The toothbrush was my one and only present.

The next five years were just more of the same. Odd kid out. I rarely got a word or gesture of kindness or caring from my stepmother.

So that's Dad's Toothbrush story. My sisters and I used to laugh and tease Dad outright when he told it, but now I understand how heartbreaking it was for him.

9

William Wesley Jones, Army Air Corps Pilot, WWII.

Well, Pop (my grandfather) came home from the trenches. He'd been mustard gassed by the Germans and suffered health problems for the rest of his life. But he and Pearl produced three daughters, and they were treated like little princesses while Dad and his brother and sisters might as well have been chained outside with the dogs.

At age 11, Dad ran away from home. In those days in Perry, Oklahoma, they didn't have many cars. In fact, they barely even had buckboards, but Dad hit the road and walked 200 miles to Humboldt, Kansas, where his uncle Joseph Brice Crawford lived. Dad loved Uncle Brice, who was just three years older than he was, and Dad named me after him. At age 16, Dad joined the National Guard and returned to Perry, where he graduated from high school in 1929, the same year Uncle Brice was accepted into West Point. Then, on October 29, the stock market crashed, and Dad dug ditches while continuing with the Guard. Wanting to follow in Uncle Brice's footsteps, he took the test to go to West Point. In 1932, when he was 21 years old, Dad beat out 44 other applicants from his district. Hell of an accomplishment for a ditch digger from Oklahoma! Upon graduation from West Point, he chose the Army Air Corps and became a pilot.

My father taught me self-reliance. Don't rely on anybody's word for things. Do it yourself, figure it out, and get it done. No excuses. And I try to live that way. The Air Force Academy reinforced it, but they didn't teach it to me initially.

My father was far and away the most significant influence in my life. Wherever or whatever I am in life, it would not have happened nearly so beneficially without the time, care, and love I was so extraordinarily lucky to receive from both my parents, especially my father. I miss him enormously and wish I had availed myself much more of him when I could have. I tell him almost daily now how much I love him, but I so wish I had told him while he was here.

Dad graduated from West Point in 1936 and married my mother in '38. I was born in December of '39.

My mother was Mary Eleanor Cutrer. Her mother's maiden name was Fithian. The Fithians were Mainliners, society muckety-mucks, from Philadelphia and New Jersey. They weren't too well-to-do, but my grandmother had an upper-crust upbringing. She married Emile Cutrer, whose family were cotton farmers from the South. They also didn't have much money, but they did have land, and some of the Cutrers went to college. One went on to become a judge. Emile, my grandfather, went to West Point. At the time, because of his exploits, he became well-known in the infantry. After about 25 years, he was medically discharged as a Lt. Colonel.

Mother was known as a "Daughter of the Infantry." She wrote her memoirs in notebooks and diaries. She had the no-

Mom teaching Brice how to dress in polite society.

tion that one day she would write a book based on her memories. She planned to call it "Aloha 'Oe—Too Many Goodbyes," subtitled "Daughter of the Infantry." It has now been published by my sister, Eleanor, who is known as "Fithian," and the book is available at Amazon.com.

My dear mother taught me the social graces, such as not to say swear words in polite conversation. She was so personable and charming. I guess when all of us are growing up, we take these things for granted. Maybe that's why we kids thought Dad's toothbrush story was so amusing. We'd always had the comfort and security of a kind and loving mother. We were a universe away from the childhood my dad had lived at our ages.

CHAPTER THREE

Marilyn Butts In

I'm Brice's sister Marilyn. From time to time I feel the need, in the interest of truth, justice, and the American way, to cast a little light on my brother's ramblings. He was just talking about our mom and how she taught him social graces, which he equates to avoiding swear words in "polite conversation." You can make a rude word count as you read his memoirs, and you'll have to conclude that he doesn't consider you, his reader, to be representative of polite society. In fact, I'll tell you what, just to spare you from the assault on your sensibilities, I'll take it upon myself to muzzle my brother. Every time you see a "bleep" you'll know that good old Marilyn is on the job.

Brice has just started this "epic" so I'm not exactly sure where he's going with it, but be warned, no matter what he feeds you, you'd best verify it with a reliable source before you chew on it.

Here's my earliest memory of my brother Brice:

Brice is about 10, and I am 4. We live in a two-story house in Arlington, Virginia. Brice is holding me by my feet, pulling me down the inside staircase, the back of my head bouncing on each step as he sings, "Seven Spoiled Brats Make Marilyn."

Yes, Brice lapped up those "social graces" Mom was teaching him.

CHAPTER FOUR
Dad's Return to Perry

It's 1954. I'm 14. The family, all six of us, Mom, Dad, the sisters and me are driving from Arlington, Virginia to Washington state where we will board a ship to Dad's next assignment in Anchorage, Alaska. Seating is a priority, the number one topic after every stop. The brass ring is "front seat by the window," the most cherished and disputed spot in Dad's Cadillac. The three remaining kids get to scramble for windows in the back seat. Being the oldest and biggest doesn't hurt my chances of avoiding the back middle.

Behind the Caddy is hitched a cool, but small camper trailer. We stay in what today you'd call RV parks most of the way. The "wide open spaces" are pretty compressed until we roll into Perry, Oklahoma, rumbling across the railroad tracks and up to Pop Jones's farm.

Then all hell breaks loose. Aunts, uncles, cousins, Pop, the dreaded Pearl, and an assortment of never-before-seen strangers engulf us, admiring the Caddy and trailer, shaking hands, slapping backs, welcoming Dad as if he's Caesar returning to Rome.

Dinner is at lunch time, supper at dinner time. Noisy is anytime. Kids are eating under the big table. Marilyn says that, under the table, a boy cousin tells her that the chicken she's eating was "jest kilt" that very morning.

Don't know how they did it, but the next day I'm on the high school stage starring as Brice the Magnificent, treating the locals to my magic show, which was funded by my paper route money and honed in the basement of our Arlington, Virginia home. The neighborhood kids back there paid two bits for 30 minutes of legerdemain and magical astonishment.

On the way back to the farmhouse, I'm wondering where Dad's toothbrush tree was. Can't tell you how Dad's stepmom Pearl or her precious daughters impressed me. All I can say is everyone seemed nice.

We'd seen Pop Jones once before, when he came to visit in Arlington. Sister Fithian thought he was a real-life cowboy who must have hitched his horse on the street. Now, he's coming down the stairs in his crowded farmhouse, a piece of burlap-rolled something under his arm. "Young Brice," he says, "step out back fer a minute."

"Yes sir."

"Seein' as how yer 14, a big fella now, I want to give you a little goin' away present. Somethin' to remind you of me." He unrolls the burlap, and there is a rifle. A real rifle!

I hold it and think—well I can't think; it's like a piece of magic out of the blue.

I must have mumbled something, because he says, "Sure, I can shoot. Fact is, shooting from the hip I can still hit a running chicken in the head."

(Wahoo!)

So we're packed in the Caddy, getting good-bye waves from the Jones bunch. Dad comes to a corner and turns left toward Alaska and the future. The other way would have taken him back the way he ran when he was 11 years old, back to Humboldt, Kansas.

CHAPTER FIVE

Brice and Dick Save the Family

It's 1955. My father is stationed at Elmendorf Air Force Base in Anchorage, Alaska. Dad and I built a cabin on Big Lake, which was about an hour's drive from Anchorage. In the summertime, we'd often fly Dad's Aeronca Chief there and land on the lake. So I learned to fly on floats.

Dad bought the plane at a yard sale. He and I stripped it down and sanded the spars, re-covered the pipe frame with new fabric and renovated it extensively. (Yes, Marilyn, in those days there were lots of fabric-covered planes.) We flew it all the time and often landed on Big Lake and spent time at our cabin. It was just great.

In the wintertime, we'd put chains on the car and drive across the frozen lake to our cabin. One time, we drove out there in the dead of winter, and I brought a friend whose name was, believe it or not, Richard Hertz.

We attached a dogsled to the car, and Dad dragged us kids around the lake. Well, this time it started snowing like crazy. We got back to the cabin to wait out the storm. Before we knew it, the snow had piled up and the car was useless. My father and mother, my three sisters and my friend and I were all snowed in. The storm eventually passed, and Dad suggested that Dick and I, who were about 15 and in good shape, "trek" back to the base and get help.

As we crossed the lake on skis, Dick and I were exhilarated, feeling like heroic adventurers off on a quest. We found a road and skied along it until, dead ahead, a big moose appeared, chugging toward us. We rolled off into a snowbank and the moose kept moving on down the road, ignoring us. Close!

We found some railroad tracks and followed them till we came upon a train stopped at a coaling or water station. The conductor agreed to give us a ride to the next town, where we found a truck driver who gave us a lift to Anchorage. From there we got a ride to the base. They cranked up a helicopter, and off we went. Dick and I were in the belly of the helicopter, a big Sikorsky H-19, with a sizeable cabin and two pilots sitting up high in the front. It was my job to guide the pilot by tapping his heel—left, right, left, right—until he found Big Lake and the cabin. The family loaded into the chopper, and we all went home.

Brice Jones and Dick Hertz saved the family. At least that's the way Dick and I saw it.

The Jones family home-built cabin,
Big Lake Alaska, 1955.

Marilyn, Eleanor and the Aeronca Chief on Big Lake, 1955.

CHAPTER SIX

No Star for Dad

It's 1956, and I'm a high school junior, a full-on self-absorbed adolescent. Of course, I feel incredibly mature. My father helped me be that way by building me up, giving me important tasks, teaching me to fly. He was always in my corner, and, of course, I took him for granted. I guess, because of his own miserable childhood, he committed himself to making sure my three sisters and I never felt insecure or unloved. Or maybe he was just that kind of man. He was totally devoted to all four of us. Of course, at the time, I assumed it was just the normal way fathers interacted with their children.

When the Japanese attacked Pearl Harbor, I had just turned two, so I have no memories of my father until he came home from the war, and then he was assigned to Okinawa as a B-29 wing commander for a couple of years. My earliest real memories of him were in Colorado Springs when I must have been about seven years old and he was assigned to the local HQ. Housing was at a premium, so for six months or so we lived in the Broadmoor Hotel, where I ran up tabs for comic books, ice cream cones, and other delights. I have a vague recollection of a day of reckoning, but it wasn't too serious, especially considering the magnitude of my crimes.

Then we moved to a ranch outside of town, where I got close to my father, camping out, hiking and riding, going up

Pikes Peak, and just in general playing around. Fast forward several years to spring of 1956. Having completed the 10th and 11th years of high school in Anchorage, it was time for my father to rotate back to the States. I was looking toward my senior year of high school, and then, I hoped, to an Academy.

Though she never outwardly complained, I knew my mother disliked living in Alaska and was anxious to get back stateside. One day before my father received his orders for his next and final duty station, he convened the family for our first, last, and only family meeting. He had been offered command of the Alaska Air National Guard. It was a Brigadier General slot, so he would receive his star, the lifelong dream of almost every career officer. He asked us all what we thought about staying a few more years in Alaska. I don't recall my sisters' exact reactions, but they weren't enthusiastic. My mother was pretty silent, but I knew how she felt, and I blurted, "No way, Dad!"

He explained that by staying he would achieve his lifelong dream, the star of a general officer. I couldn't have cared less. "We wanna go back to the States!"

True to my father's extraordinary commitment to his family, that's what we did.

Today, I am so ashamed of my spoiled, selfish behavior, I almost want to cry. I know if I had been in Dad's shoes, I would have just explained to the family that our next assignment was in Juneau, where I would be the Guard Commander.

If we had stayed, I could still have gone to an Academy after a year in Juneau, my mother and sisters would have got through a couple more years in Alaska, my father would retire, and they'd all move to the States. But to please his family, he requested duty in Southern California, where his only brother lived, and he took a (bleep) assignment as commander of a supply depot. We moved into a home in Garden Grove, California. Dad commuted an hour each way every day, in awful traffic (for the times), and after a couple of years running the supply depot, he retired at age 50 with over 28 years of service and set up a real estate shop.

CHAPTER SEVEN

Balls

In 1956, after Alaska, my father took his last assignment. The Southern California public schools weren't so hot back then, so, in order to get me into a military academy, Dad made a financial sacrifice and sent me down the coast toward San Diego to a military prep school in Carlsbad, the Army and Navy Academy. They made an exception and accepted me in my final year. They would have been right not to take me since I was a dedicated screw-up and ended up on probation not once, but four times. Quadruple Probation! For some reason, that makes me a bit proud. They would have thrown me out, but they were pretty sure I was going to get into an academy, and that would have been a feather in their cap because as a military prep school they needed to show parents they could get their kid into an academy, and they didn't have too many hopefuls because a large number of their students were spoiled rich kids from Hollywood, or sad offspring of self-absorbed parents who couldn't be bothered with them.

I can't say that was the case with a classmate I became good friends with, Wade Davis. His parents did have money, though, and they lived in Beverly Hills. Wade had been at the academy from eighth grade through this, his and my senior year. He knew his way around that school.

I didn't have a nickel, but I was kind of a screw-up, and Wade liked being associated with screw-ups, apparently. One night, we crept out of our rooms at 2 a.m., bent on doing mischief.

The administration building was near the tennis courts and had a high flat roof. Wade knew all the doors and stairwells and how to access them in the dead of night, so up we went, all the way to the roof. There were more than a hundred tennis balls up there, strays from the tennis courts down below. We hunkered down behind a little parapet that ran around the roof perimeter, and we scanned the terrain. Not a living soul moving down there, but, oh wait, shambling along, the night watchman, Major Trainor, a real major in the Army reserves, approached, making his rounds. Opportunity called. Stationed on the high ground, out of view of the unsuspecting target, we had the perfect setup to test the tenets of successful military tactics as laid out in *Combat Operations, Strategies for Interdiction*, Volume III, page 409. From our height, we could sling tennis balls a great distance. Major Trainor never knew where they were coming from. We did this for months. Poor guy. Oh God, that was fun though.

Well, in spite of my four probations, I did get into the Air Force Academy, but not because of the Army and Navy Academy, but because my father pulled some strings.

CHAPTER EIGHT

Depth Perception

I played sports growing up. Around fifth grade, I was in Little League. I was an excellent first baseman, I thought, but I couldn't hit. In high school, I still couldn't hit, but I made the team because I had fancy footwork on first base and understood the position. But believe me, a lot of fun goes out of baseball if you can't hit.

I didn't figure out my hitting problem till I was 25 years old and playing on an Air Force softball team. I broke down everything I was doing in the batter's box and realized that standing sideways to the pitched ball and following its flight to the catcher's mitt required something I didn't have: depth perception. I opened up my stance so I was pretty much looking at the ball face on and could see it all the way with both eyes. Then I began to hit the ball, and I was a pretty damned good ball player. But I was 25, too late to be Stan Musial.

Having no depth perception complicated my life as a pilot.

More about that later.

CHAPTER NINE

A Warm Welcome

When I got to the Air Force Academy in July of '57, it was still located at the "temporary site" at Lowry Air Force Base in Denver. The "permanent site" in the foothills north of Colorado Springs was under construction and a year away from opening. We, the class of 1961, only the third class admitted to the Air Force Academy, were the freshmen. The classes of '59 and '60 were juniors and sophomores.

The first couple of days at the Academy, our incoming class was hassled, screamed at, chewed out, slammed to attention, made to perform endless pushups, head-shaved, run into the ground, required to verbally inform upperclassmen that we had or had not performed a bowel movement in the past 24 hours, and, in general, received the treatment the Indians accorded Custer's soldiers at the Little Bighorn.

My classmate Lee Butler tells this story: It was our first or second day, and we're out on the ramp, in formation, getting our chins rammed in, and suddenly there's a SPLAT! And a CRASH! Something hitting the ramp, followed by the yell of an upperclassman on the second floor of one of the white clapboard barracks that served as Cadet Quarters during USAFA's stay at Lowry Air Force Base. The upperclassman had just thrown an electric razor found in a Doolie's room inspection, down onto the ramp, yelling, "We don't need no 'lectric razors 'round here!" Welcome to the Air Force Academy.

CHAPTER TEN
Honor Code

The Air Force Academy Honor Code was, "We will not lie, cheat, or steal, nor tolerate among us those who do." And there was no forgiveness, no discretion, no nothin'. It was black or white. And if you saw an honor violation, you were honor bound to turn it in. If you didn't, you were guilty of an honor violation yourself.

In our very first academic month, a classmate was picking up exam papers for the instructor, and he was sort of glancing at them as he did so. Two desks away from me, he looked at one of the papers and he, aww (bleep)! He put the paper back down, and on his own paper he erased and rewrote his answer. Clearly cheating! You know, twenty years later they wouldn't have thrown the guy out for that. They would have given him what they call "discretion," taught him a lesson, and I think that would have been the right thing to do.

Anyway, I turned him in because I was honor bound to do so, and he met an honor panel, and they voted to throw him out of the Academy.

Well, it didn't bother me too much because an honor violation is an honor violation is an honor violation, and we all knew what the deal was. I had to do it. I can almost think of the guy's name. He came by my room as he was checking out of the Academy at Lowry and said, "Don't give it another thought, Brice.

26

You did what you had to do, and I don't hold it against you." He forgave me, and I thought, well, that was very nice of him, but, you know, I was too blasé about it. I didn't understand that I could have been ruining his life. I hope I didn't ruin it. Guys left the Academy all the time and went on to college and had decent lives, but it could have ruined his life. It probably would have ruined my life if I was in his shoes. It would have at least, sure as hell changed it. But now when I think of that incident, I think how wrong it was to not have a little discretion. I mean, let the guy learn his lesson.

Chapter Eleven

Doolies

Freshmen were known as fourth-classmen, or "doolies," which translates to, "those upon whom the (bleep) that rolls downhill comes to rest."

We had to double-time everywhere. When questioned, there were only three correct responses: yes sir, no sir, and no excuse sir. We ate while sitting at attention and only when given permission by an upperclassman.

At the end of first semester we got to choose our roommates, and Rich Mayo, Academy quarterback of the number 6 rated college football team in the nation and I had chosen to room together, but the upperclassmen made me room with a guy who was the most unmilitary cadet in the squadron. Mayo drew another guy who was not much better. We were supposed to shape them up. On top of his Gomer Pyle-like failings in the military arena, my screw-up roommate managed to fail math. He had to take the course over again in the summer. He somehow powered himself through the entire four years at the Academy, but he never did shape up on the military front. I think they picked the wrong guy (me) to shape him up. But I really did grow fond of him, and we remain close friends today.

Tom Pattie was a year ahead of us, and, therefore, an officially designated "upperclassman," which translates to "guy who is licensed to torment freshmen." But Tom was more of a mischief-maker than a hazer. He had a motorcycle secretly stored on base, and he made it available to me and my roommate, Brusk. That was quite a luxury being able to get off base at Lowry at midnight or 2 a.m. to go to Bob's Big Boy for a hamburger. But beware Tom Pattie bearing gifts.

One night I woke up with a shiver. I was wet and getting wetter. "Damn, it's raining in here," I yelled.

Brusk, my roommate, shouted "Shut up!" from the other side of the room.

I grabbed the wastebasket off the floor by my bed and held it over my chest. Drip, drip, into the wastebasket. "It's still doing it," I complained.

"Why don't you move your bed?"

Duh! Problem solved.

Okay, I admit it. Brusk may have had more common sense than I did.

Drip, drip, drip. The sound from the wastebasket continued. Tom Pattie, whose room was right above ours, had drilled a hole in the floor directly above my bed and put a towel around the hole and was pouring water on it all night long. Unbelievable.

A highlight of our first year was 60th Day. For one day, one special day, 60 days before the end of the 1957-58 school year, we the doolies (freshmen) exchanged places (roles) with the much-despised class of 1960 and got to lord it over them. We could haze them for one day and make their lives miserable, as they had done to us since our Academy time began.

I had a blank check to get even with Tom Pattie! While he was getting hazed by my fellow doolies, I went upstairs to his room and poured molasses down the barrel of his rifle, into the magazine and so forth. Remember, he was an upperclassman at that time. That'll teach him a lesson, I thought. I also had liberated a meringue pie from the mess hall, thinking it might come in handy on this day of mischief.

I was in the dorm hallway, pie in hand, when along came Pattie, all dressed up, looking smart in his uniform. I stood him at attention and liberally applied meringue to his blouse (uniform jacket). Of course, Tom Pattie's mind was one step ahead of mine. He had swapped his rifle for mine the day before 60th Day. And he was wearing my blouse!

CHAPTER TWELVE
Press-on's Pants

In the summer of '58, the cadets marched into the brand new "permanent site." Gleaming aluminum and glass ultra-modern buildings, grouped around a huge "terrazzo." Our home for the next three years.

When they built the Air Force Academy, they must have thought a monumentally high flagpole was needed to fit into the towering Rampart Range of the Rockies. Monuments can be built to honor heroic deeds. Monuments can also inspire certain individuals to perform heroic deeds. One such deed follows:

Late one night, I hear a knock on my door. Tom Pattie stands there, holding Major "Press-on" Smith's pants. Major Smith's moniker attached to him because he was famous for saying, "press on" as cadets' backs hit the wall (slamming to attention) as he walked by. When on duty, the designated Officer of the Day spends the night in what is called "Security Flight," and "Press-on" is Officer of the Day. Cadet Tom Pattie has successfully sneaked into Security Flight and requisitioned the sleeping Press-on's trousers. Now he's in my doorway, Doolie Wacker, the equivalent of Batman's Robin, alongside him. It's about two in the morning, and they want to run Press-on's pants up the 100-foot flagpole. And I'm invited to participate.

Well, we start by tying the flagpole rope around Pattie's middle and hoisting him up. At about 20 feet, Tom is being cut in half by the rope. He's gagging, can't talk. We figure we'd better lower him before he expires. Doolie Wacker runs off and comes back with a canteen belt. We put it on Pattie and tie the rope to the belt. Tom is lifted 100 feet into the night sky. He ties the pants to the ball at the top of the pole. We lower him down, and the next morning, Press-on calls his wife for another pair of pants. He keeps the entire cadet wing standing at attention out on the terrazzo, under his flapping pants. Eventually, he has to let us go to breakfast, but not before he announces that unless the guilty parties come forward, there will be severe consequences. (What a numb-nut.)

The pants fly proudly over cadet formations for four or five days because the Air Force doesn't have anything to take them down with. They have to go to Fort Carson to get a crane that can lift a guy high enough to remove Press-on's pants.

CHAPTER THIRTEEN
The Great Mule Raid

September 1959. The first USAFA class had graduated in June. Now we were juniors, second classmen. Tom Pattie, having flunked some academic course or other, had been "turned back" from the class of '60 to our class, the class of '61, to repeat the academic year, so he was now my classmate rather than my upperclassman, and we became co-conspirators in the Great Mule Raid, the plan to kidnap Westpoint's mascot.

Mule Raiders

(Front): Ken MacAulay, Tom Pattie.
(Rear): Marty Fricks, Jerry Mason, Bill Foster,
Brice, Wayne Whalen.

We added a few members to our raiding party, and, unfortunately, we kept adding till there were eleven. Way too many. And our scheme was way too elaborate.

Being a member of the 4th Cadet Squadron, I phoned the Air Force unit that sponsored us, the 4th Tactical Airlift Squadron, in North or South Carolina as I recall. I told them what we needed, and they sent not one but two C-130s out to Peterson Field in Colorado Springs to take us to the base near West Point, where we landed on Friday night, 25 Sep 59.

We planned to spend Friday night reconnoitering at West Point. So before we left Colorado, I went to Fort Carson Army Base just a few miles from Pete Field in Colorado Springs and picked up four walkie talkies, which were really large in those days, well over a foot long with even longer antennas.

When the C-130s landed near West Point, we stayed at a doolie's house in Highland Falls, just outside the south gate of West Point. The doolie was part of the crew because of his home's location, plus his family provided some wheels. When we got there, we rented two panel trucks with loading ramps. This was my idea. Way too complicated.

The plan was we'd load the mule into one of the trucks, which looked different from one another, and since there were military mule-keepers living in the mule barracks building, I figured they might see us loading the mule into the one truck and be looking for that one. But we'd switch the mule to the other truck at a predetermined location on West Point's grounds. So the new truck would get out the gate without being stopped. In retrospect it sounds silly, but that was the plan.

Here's how it all unfolded. Or, to be honest, folded.

Friday Night Reconnoiter: We had to verify where the mule was, how we'd get to it, spring it, and safely extract it from the enemy's clutches. Feeling excited and not a little bit scared, we left the doolie's house and fanned out, seeking tactical info.

After we located the mule barracks and decided on an escape route, one of our number, Tom Pattie, in fact, ever the non-conformist, expanded his reconnaissance to include a cadet dorm, which he entered around 2 a.m., emerging before 3 carrying a full West Point cadet uniform, complete from the cap right down to the shoes.

Brice with Walkie-Talkie and Tom Pattie at West Point, standing next to rented Mule Truck.

As a fashion accessory, he had also liberated a company guidon, a small flag on a pole, used in marching formations.

Saturday, 26 Sep 59 (D-Day): In the morning, we went back to West Point to watch the Saturday morning parade. We gathered on a sidewalk and watched as, down the street from the dorm area, drums rattling, marched the US Military Cadet Corps, the "Long Gray Line," and at the back of one of the companies, looking smart in his purloined uniform, marched Tom Pattie, right under our noses! He didn't have a rifle, but he sure as hell looked like he belonged. The West Point cadets marched onto the parade grounds, and Tom marched with them through the whole parade and into the Cadet Mess Hall. He had lunch with the West Point cadets! When I asked him how he got away with it, he said, "I just went along with what the others were doing."

The year before, Army's football team had gone undefeated, and their star, Pete Dawkins, had won the Heisman trophy as the best college football player in America. So for their first game of 1959, expectations in West Point were high. That afternoon, Army defeated Boston College 44-8, and the entire school and community went bananas as daylight fled and the intrepid mule raiders lurked, waiting to strike.

Night fell, West Point partied, the raiders, now dressed in black, armed themselves with the necessities: flashlights, huge military-issue walkie talkies, crash-crew bolt cutters, and whatever else we could think of.

Our convoy deployed two panel trucks with loading ramps and one four-door sedan. Ken MacAulay drove the relief truck and parked out of sight. The other truck carried us to the mule barracks and backed up to the door. Silently, we slipped inside. It was dark, but as our eyes adjusted, we could see there were about a dozen stalls. Odors of manure, hay, and the mules themselves hung in the air. We picked a stall, cut the lock off with the crash-crew cutters, opened the gate, and there stood one damned big mule, towering over Wayne Whalen. Bells and alarms started clanging and wailing, lights came on flashing red and white, and the mule was scared shitless, shaking its head and stomping. Some men ran in, not military police, but mule caretakers. They had been celebrating West Point's victory and were drunk as skunks. When they saw all these guys dressed in black, holding walkie-talkies and crash crew cutters, they froze. Whalen grabbed the mule by his halter and tried to get him up the truck ramp. The mule had other ideas.

Then Marty Fricks, another key member of the Great Mule Raid team, the man who single-handedly fashioned in the Academy's electrical engineering lab a 440-volt hot-stick, decided the time was right for the heroic launch of his diabolical invention. Marty had a packet about the size of two books attached to a strap slung over his shoulder. From the power packet a wire and a wand extended. He strode to the mule and stuck his magic wand right in his butt. Oh (bleep), I can't not laugh when I picture that pivotal event.

Four hundred forty volts went through that mule. It took off across the field and parking lot, Whalen bravely hanging on to its halter. More than a hundred yards were crossed before the mule finally slowed down. Well, the Great Raid fell apart. It was every man for himself. Alarms were sounding, lights were flashing everywhere, and we had to get back to the doolie's house.

Muleless.

We had a car and the other truck stashed on West Point's grounds, but never mind, we piled into the truck and headed for the gate.

But remember MacAulay? He was waiting at our Mule Transfer Checkpoint, sitting behind the wheel of truck number two, and the way he tells it, "I was sitting in the driver's seat staring ahead, out the windshield, when I felt cold steel behind my ear, and a voice said, 'Move, and you're dead.'" It was an MP.

So they got MacAulay. The rest of us arrived safely back at the doolie's house. We were jammed in there, adrenaline racing, when a taxicab pulled up. The driver got out and walked to the door. We never figured out how he knew where to go, but on his dispatch radio he relayed messages back and forth between us and the "authorities" for hours. There were no cell phones back then, of course, and the walkie-talkies were on our frequency, not theirs. The MPs didn't want egg on their faces for what happened on their watch, so they were doing the negotiating. Their "final offer" boiled down to, "Either all you guys turn yourselves in (they didn't know how many we were) or we're going to throw your buddy down one of our tunnels." (West Point had a bunch of tunnels between various buildings like the Mess Hall and the dorms.)

"We're going to keep MacAulay down there till the Army-Air Force football game." Well, that game was on 31 October, more than a month away. So, of course, we turned ourselves in.

After taking names and gloating, they let us all go.

On Sunday morning, when we got back to the waiting C-130s, the pilots were all disappointed. The mule they were ready to transport was conspicuously absent. The fact that Tom Pattie was carrying the appropriated guidon was small consolation. Really, all we had to show for the Great Raid was that guidon.

We landed back at Pete Field pretty much empty-handed and despondent. But what an adventure! A lot more exciting than the next year when we went to Annapolis and successfully stole the Navy goat. But by then we had learned our lesson: Keep the number of raiders down, and keep the plan simple.

CHAPTER FOURTEEN
Honor Code Revisited

One of the things I want to catch up on is the honor violation. My experience with the guy I had to turn in (I think his name was Weldon) was painful eventually, but there was another experience that was painful instantly. It was an "all right sir" event in my senior year. "All right sir" means, "I don't have the missing articles that had been posted on each academy bulletin board in the Cadet Quarters, informing us that there is going to be an "all right" inspection for the lost articles. So as the official inquisitor goes from room to room, an "all right, sir" from each room in response to a knock on the cadet's room door means, "I don't have the articles, and I have checked my footlocker in the trunk room down in the basement."

So after one of these inspections, a kid turned himself in saying, "I didn't have the articles, but I did not check my locker. I knew I didn't have them, but I didn't go down to the basement and check. And saying, 'all right, sir' meant I had gone down and checked."

That was a knife in my heart because I don't know how many cadets ever went down and checked their stupid footlockers for somebody's overcoat or whatever was missing. I don't know that I did. And the kid turned himself in. He was a stellar cadet, great guy. I knew who he was. I had him in a 4th class training session when I was a senior. He was a great kid with a lot of potential. He turned himself in and they said, "Well, there's not a lot to discuss here. You're kicked out." And he left.

Boy, that hurt, and I said, "Something's gotta be done about it because this is just not right." And, of course, as the years went by, the Academy instituted a policy of "discretion," where there were other remedies such as turning back the offender to the next year's class. I was talking to somebody in the wine business recently who said he knew of a guy who had been turned back for an honor violation. And I thought, well, even turning back a year is just kinda like vengeance. I don't think it makes any sense. Give the guy some discretion. Let him learn from his mistake.

So that incident really, really, really got to me personally, and, frankly, I don't think I went down and checked my locker most of the time, and I don't know if anyone else did.

Chapter Fifteen

The Goat

Now it's the end of the summer of 1960, and Tom Pattie (what a man) has the idea that we should go get the Navy Goat. We have the failed mule experience under our belts from the year before, so we build on that. This time, there are but three of us, Pattie, Wayne Whalen, and yours truly.

Pattie comes from Maryland. He has family there. We hitch a ride there on a military flight. The Naval Academy has a farm outside Annapolis where they keep their three goats during the summer. Tom borrows the family car, and we drive to the farm late Saturday night (Sunday morning), intending to steal a goat right away. But it's a real working dairy farm with cows and all, and it's crawling with people working at 3 in the morning. So now we know that farmers, especially dairy farmers, go to work very early. But we see the lay of the land, leave, and come back at 11 p.m. Nobody there. The silence is broken only by an occasional cow fart. We find the goat in a little hut with a fence around it. Whalen jumps right over the fence. I'll never forget the vision of that kid launching his skinny ass up and over the fence without a second's hesitation. He was the first guy in with the mule, and, by God, he's first in with the goat. In later years, Wayne will be a very successful litigator in Chicago, and he'll pack on a lot of successful lawyer poundage. But back in the summer of 1960, he floats right over the rail, all fearless attitude and ninja grace. The goat bursts out of his little hut, and Wayne chases him down and tackles him. Pattie jumps the fence and hogties the goat while Wayne holds him down. I'm still outside the fence, just watching. I have no desire to touch that creature. But the three of us carry the goat out to Tom's car and put him in the trunk. The next morning, we look at each other and say, "What do we do now?" We never thought about the return.

So here's my chance to be more than dead weight. I think I know the base commander at Andrews Air Force Base. When I was about 14, in Alaska, the colonels' quarters were duplexes, and the guy who lived next door to us was Col. Smith, who I had heard is now the base commander at Andrews. So we drive Pattie's car out there with the goat still in the trunk, find base HQ, and I go in.

"Is Col. Smith the base commander?"

"Yes, he is."

"Well, I'd like to see him."

I wait for 20 minutes and a sergeant ushers me in. Col. Smith walks from behind his desk and extends a friendly hand.

"Hey, Brice, good to see you, I hear you're at the Academy now."

"That's right, sir. I'm a cadet there."

"Well, it's great to see you. What brings you out here?"

"Well, sir, we've got the Navy goat in a car in the parking lot."

"You WHAT?"

"Yes, sir. Do you think we could commandeer an airplane back to the Academy?"

Eventually, he comes down off the ceiling and says, "Meet me at the flight line in an hour."

An hour later, we're at the flight line. Col. Smith has requisitioned a B-26. Think WWII, two big prop engines and a bomb bay. And two pilots. A veterinarian, standing there with a hypodermic needle about two-feet long, sticks it in the goat. Goat's eyeballs roll back in his skull. He goes limp. We hoist him on a rope and a pulley into the bomb bay. It occurs to me if the pilot pushes a button it can be "goats away" over Missouri. So with goat in bay, Tom, Wayne, and I wedge into accessible spaces. We're off to Colorado.

Back in Colorado Springs, Tom says, "I know a master sergeant with a farm near here." Probably where Tom stashes his illegal motorcycle. So the master sergeant agrees to keep the goat on his farm. The plan, if you can call it that, is to keep him there till the Air Force-Navy football game, months hence.

The Navy goes berserk looking for their goat, and we speculate they had early warning satellite imagery, because, somehow they had the license plate number on Tom's folks' car. With that, even the US Navy could figure out at least one of the culprits. So the Navy calls the Academy superintendent, who calls in Tom Pattie. And the Supe says, "Produce it." The deal is, nothing will happen if we turn ourselves in and give 'em back the goat. So we produce it with its horns painted Air Force blue. At a lunch formation we march him down to the mess hall, and Billy is returned to the Navy. Have no idea how Billy got to Annapolis, but he did.

Life magazine gave it a nice spread. Wayne and I got our names and pictures in it, and Tom Pattie wasn't even mentioned. The article was based on an "interview" an Academy PR guy conducted with the goat. Tom never showed up for it.

Typical of the guy. Never showed his face, never took any credit. As far as *Life* was concerned, Wayne Whalen and I were the only perpetrators—which is kinda the way Tom liked it.

Eventually, Navy made a raid on our falcons and took one, but it was a year after the big football game had already been played. No big deal, but eventually, like 40-some years later, one dark night before a Navy/AF football game, they painted our static F-4 display aircraft on our campus as a Blue Angels plane. Now that was a class act!

Billy being interiewed by Hector Negroni as
Wayne Whalen and Brice look on.

CHAPTER SIXTEEN

A Class 2 Violation

It's the summer of 1960. The classes of 1959 and 1960 have both graduated. We, the class of '61, are now First Classmen, seniors, top dogs. I've made it through three years without a single offense other than minor demerit infractions, which everyone gets from time to time. To put this in perspective, Robert E. Lee is the *only* West Pointer in history to have graduated without a single demerit. Of course, he never had Tom Pattie for a mentor.

To be honest, Tom wasn't even involved in the offense that earned me a face-to-face with the Commandant of Cadets. It was a *Class 2 Violation*. (Drum roll, please.)

As the new first classmen, we were in charge of training the incoming doolie class. My roommate at the time was Leroy McCleskey, a Georgia boy, and we were both assigned to work on the obstacle course. Mac was stationed in a copse of trees located next to "the pit," a maliciously designed hole about twelve feet wide, full of water, with a rope hanging down in the middle. You'd run up to the pit, lunge at the rope, swing and, in theory, land safe and dry on the other side. But the devious bastards who designed the pit made the opposite side about 18 inches higher than the side you leapt off from, and there were boards facing the runner so the poor doolies would run up to the pit, lunge, grab the rope, hit the boards on the other side and fall into the water, most of the time. McCleskey made sure they fell in all of the time. He was hidden in the trees, and, as the dool-ies lunged for the rope, he'd fire off ten rounds of blanks on a 50 caliber machine gun and scare the living (bleep) out of the poor kids, so if they didn't hit the board and fall off it would be because they'd missed the rope altogether when the rounds went off.

Well, I decided I was going to teach McCleskey a lesson, so I grabbed a doolie running the obstacle course and said, "Listen, here's what's gonna happen. You're gonna lunge at the rope, a machine gun's gonna go off, and you're gonna fall into the pit, screaming *aaaaahh*, and you're gonna float face down like you've been shot. See?"

The kid was great. He lunged. Gun went off. *Brrrrrrrrrpp*. Kid goes *aaaaahh*, falls face down and floats. I run up there and shout, "McCleskey, he's been hit!"

This was going to be the end of it as I dragged him out of the pit, but the officer in charge of the obstacle course, 2nd Lt. Sutton, maybe three years older than we were, arrived just as the *brrrrrrrpp—aaaaahh* scenario played out.

I'm pulling the kid from the water when Sutton says, "What's the matter? What's the—"

"He's been hit sir!"

"Oh my God!" Sutton runs and gets his car, a VW bug. We load the kid into the right seat. Sutton gets behind the wheel. The kid's moaning and groaning.

Sutton drives as fast as his bug can go, across athletic fields making tracks in the grass, and praying aloud, "God, please don't let him die," and the kid is slumping over the gearshift going *aaaaahh*.

Finally, Sutton drives across a freshly laid lawn right to the door of the dispensary, pulls the kid out, drags him through the door yelling, "He's been shot!"

They lay the kid on a table, cut his clothes off, look him over and say, "Where are you hit?"

At that point, the kid sits up and says, "Well, I'm not really hit, sir."

So, I was invited to meet the Commandant, but, as it turned out, I never actually got to meet him, because, apparently, he was busy laughing his ass off. They didn't know what to charge me with, so they put their heads together and came up with "unauthorized assumption of authority" and gave me a Class 2, which meant confinement to my room for six weeks.

That was my only offense at the Academy resulting in more than demerits. Never walked a "tour," just got confinement.

In aviation circles this is called "flying under the radar."

CHAPTER SEVENTEEN

Monte

A word about roommates. Monte Moorberg was my room-mate 3rd class year (sophomore) and 1st class year (senior). In junior year, I drew McCleskey. It was kinda like getting Brusk at the time. Mac was deemed to need bucking up (ha-ha). Monte and I wanted to room together, but they split us up. So I drew McCleskey and, like Brusk, grew to like him a lot. Great guy.

Monte and I roomed together two years, and even when we were separated for junior year, we did everything together. We came to California on vacation together. We did field trips together. We went everywhere together. It got to be a joke around the squadron. Tweedledee and Tweedledum. We'd amble out to formations side-by-side. We'd do everything together. When we graduated, he was number 127 in the class order of merit, and I was number 128. We stood side-by-side at the graduation, and I followed him up to get the diploma. It was incredible after those three years of doing everything side-by-side.

Monte outranked me most of the time. He was a more splendid cadet. Senior year he was made squadron commander.

Monte got married right after graduation, and he asked me to be best man. At his wedding rehearsal dinner in Grand Island, Nebraska, Monte introduced me as, "Brice Jones, just one man dumber than me." Brought the house down.

Graduation, 1961.
Monte Moorberg is on the left, third row (cast on right hand).
Brice is next to him, "Just one man dumber…"

CHAPTER EIGHTEEN
Tom

Maybe a word now on Tom Pattie. He was always in the 4th Squadron, just like Monte and me. Even though he'd been turned back from the class of '60 to our class of '61, on the "Screw Your Buddy" sheets, our cadet peer ratings, he did very well (we all loved him), so he was made the squadron commander first semester of senior year. But he was Tom Pattie, and he just had to play outside the lines. He managed to get his ass in a crack with his anti-establishment pranks and got busted all the way down from cadet colonel to basic cadet, from four stripes on his shoulder boards (epaulettes) to none. To put that in perspective, the only cadets with no rank on their shoulder boards were doolies, freshmen. Tom was a senior; in fact, he was in his fifth year as an Air Force Academy cadet. Now he was no longer squadron commander, no longer a cadet colonel but a lowly "basic" cadet. The lowest of the low, which meant a lot more to everyone else than it did to Tom.

Upon graduation, Tom went to the Army. Should have gone Marines. He was certainly tough and fearless. In Vietnam, he was severely injured by a landmine. I haven't seen him since then, but I heard he limps quite badly.

Tom Pattie and Jerry Mason, fellow mule raiders at West Point. Tom is wearing his "borrowed" West Point uniform.

CHAPTER NINETEEN
From Graduation to Vietnam

In June of 1961, we graduated, freshly minted second lieu-
tenants. Two classmates and I had planned to take a trip to
South America for 30 days before reporting to our first duty
assignment. We'd all taken Spanish in school and got pretty
good at it. I'd never been to South America, although I'd moved
around a lot to other places in the States. The other two guys
crapped out, and I decided to do it myself. Took off on military
space available ("Space A") and flew down to Panama, where I
was born. Saw the Canal. Then Space A on down to Lima, Peru,
traveled through Chile and Argentina, then up to Rio, where I
ran out of money. My second lieutenant's pay of $222 a month
wasn't keeping up with my lifestyle.

Somehow, I got on a military line and called my father.

"Dad, could you call my bank in Colorado Springs and just
ask them to drop about $300 into my bank account, and I'll fill
out the loan papers and so forth, but I'm out of money and I
need about $300 to make it back."

Dad gets back to me. "Your bank doesn't think you're man-
aging your money well, so they turned you down."

This was my first lesson in not spending money when I
don't have any, especially if I'm wandering in foreign places. It
was also my first lesson in "dork sitting at desks." By the way,
I'm only saying "dorks" so Marilyn doesn't bleep the real word.

(More on that later.) So, anyway, I'm broke. We didn't have credit cards or cell phones in those days.

I can remember going to the fanciest Copcabana Beach restaurant, thatched huts and all that, flaming grills at every table. Argentine beef broiled and served on the spot. It was fabulous, except I'm all alone at a table, with eleven cents in my pocket. I wangle a plate of french fries.

Somehow, I scrounged a military flight home, and I was off to pilot training at Webb Air Force Base in Big Spring, Texas. A lot of guys went to bases near their hometowns. I didn't have a hometown, but Webb had just received the brand-new Northrop T-38 Talon, the world's first supersonic jet trainer.

So who do you suppose was in my pilot training class at Webb? My permanently un-military Academy roommate, whom I never could "buck up," that's who. So, for all my savvy, I was no better off than Brusk!

I graduated in the T-38 either at the top of the class in flying, or second in flying, and either last or next to last in academics and military training.

They weighted those three equally, so I graduated two thirds of the way down. I didn't have to take a helicopter or a B-52, but I did end up drawing a C-124, along with several other guys, Brusk included. That was okay. It was not the end of the world. It was a fine airplane. Sort of. But the mission of that airplane was to travel the world. OK for a while.

The last night at Webb Air Force Base, though, our class bachelors had quite a party in the BOQ (Bachelor Officers' Quarters). We were all completely drunk. I went over to the mess hall as the sun was rising and lifted a whole big steamer tray of scrambled eggs and scuttled back to Randy Kennedy's BOQ room. My stupefied classmates proceeded to throw the eggs all over the lawn. Randy pitched in and threw his desk over the railing. As the Air Police drove up, probably responding to a call about noise and mayhem, everybody yelled *bleep yous* and scattered to the wind.

Well, almost everybody. Randy Kennedy was beyond stupefied and we had stuck him in the shower. Somebody, Brusk claims it was him, dragged him out of the shower and dressed him in a flight suit, over his wet pajamas. There followed The Day of Hiding Randy.

Randy was in the next graduating class after us, so he hadn't graduated and had to report for flying that morning. Brusk drove him down to the flight line, pointed him in the direction of the flight shack, and told him to inform his instructor that he was too sick to fly. He was so wasted he had to walk sideways, leaning hand-over-hand on the walls for support. Obviously, he couldn't report on sick call that way, so we stashed him in an ambulance next to the hospital. A medic who found the whole thing amusing helped out. But Randy was nowhere to be found as far as the brass was concerned. Missing in action.

Anyway, when it all got sorted out, I got a "referral" ER, which is a very bad report on my conduct. I had to report to my first duty station, Donaldson Air Force Base, in Greenville, South Carolina, with that as the first rating in my personnel folder. Brusk got a referral ER too, but it meant nothing to him, just another brick in the wall. I reported in with this ER firmly attached to my ass. So, my flying career was off to a roaring start.

And I was flying C-124s, Douglas Globemasters, 200 knots on a good day, 10,000 feet altitude. Not so lovingly referred to as "Old Shakey" or the "Aluminum Overcast." From supersonic jet at 40,000 feet to four piston propeller engines, flying about as slow as a plane that size could go without falling out of the sky. But, we did fly around the world in them and saw lots of interesting places.

Brice and C-124 wheel. The photo was meant to be a joke. Obviously, you don't need a g suit, helmet, or scarf to fly "Old Shakey."

As soon as I got to Donaldson and checked in, they sent me to Reno for survival training. Then they closed Donaldson, and we all moved to Hunter Air Force Base in Savannah, Georgia. We rented a beach house on Tybee Island. Larry Shoemaker, Roger Stringer, me, and Brusk. Lot of fun.

Roger Stringer got ill coming back on a trip in the Pacific, and checked in to Tripler Army Hospital in Honolulu. He had a painful sore inside his mouth. He never got out of the hospital, though he was transferred to Walter Reed in Washington, until he died a few months later with cancer of the jaw. By then, they had cut away half his face.

Dear Roger. We buried him in '64. Gee, he was a brilliant guy. He was going to go to Georgetown. He could have been Secretary of State, or any damn thing he wanted. He was just great. He loved international affairs. Quite the man. After we'd been flying around the world for six months, he said, "You know, Brice, we ought to write a book about our world travels. We can title it, *"Snack Bars and Runways I Have Seen."* He was very cool.

So there I was, flying C-124s out of Savannah, Georgia, and you know, it was OK for a while because we were going to Czechoslovakia, Rome, Athens, and other interesting places and seeing the world. But after a year or so that engine noise was getting to me. The C-124 had four Pratt and Whitney R4360 engines, the largest displacement aviation piston engines to be mass-produced in the United States, and probably the loudest. The pilots couldn't talk to one another, they had to communicate through headphones, or, when necessary, scream.

I called my father and griped. He said, "You ought to enjoy it, because you'll stand out from all those other weenies flying 124s."

Well, Dad couldn't help me, so I called Lieutenant Colonel Kenneth Tallman, who was our first group AOC at the Academy. I didn't know him from squat. After his stint at the Academy, he had been assigned to the Pentagon.

"Colonel Tallman, I gotta get out of here. I can't do this anymore."

"Who is this again?"

"I was in the First Group at the Academy, you know: 'Fightin' 4th Squadron,' and you were our group AOC."

"Oh yeah, sure."

He didn't remember me for sour owl-*bleep*. Of course not. Every cadet looks the same, with their white sidewall haircuts and uniforms. So he says, "Well, Lt. Jones, would you go to Vietnam?"

"Yes sir."

Couple of days later, he calls back. "Sorry, Lt. Jones, Vietnam is a blue-ribbon program, (They only took volunteers back then, in the early years.) and frankly your last ER, oh..."

Well, I blah-blah-blahed my ass off, and within a week or two he got me an assignment in C-47s.

The C-47 is a tail-dragging "Gooney Bird," the military version of the venerable DC-3, just about the most archaic flying machine both then and now.

"Yessir, I'll take a C-47." It's not as if I was going to get a fighter aircraft with my dubious record.

CHAPTER TWENTY
His Honor in Pink

I'm on my way. It's 19 December 1964, and I'm done with C-124s. Going to Vietnam to fly C-47s. Driving Highway 80 in my '57 Thunderbird all the way from Savannah, Georgia to Newport Beach, California, where I'll spend Christmas and New Year's with my parents, then get my ass up to Travis Air Force Base via Sacramento and catch my flight to Vietnam on 6 January.

Zipping along Highway 80 at 3 o'clock in the morning, the right seat is graced by my lovely traveling companion. Of course, OEM for a '57 T-Bird is a comely blonde. Don't believe me? Look it up in the owner's manual.

Up ahead is a stoplight. The not-so-cosmopolitan burg of Gooberville, Georgia lies dead ahead. The road is dark and empty. The stop light is green, but just as I hit the intersection it turns red, and, of course, there's a cop on the cross street. *Aaaargh!* He pulls me over.

"Boy, you done run a red light."

"It was green when I got there."

"No. It was red."

He has me follow him back to the courthouse. I leave the blonde in the right seat and follow him up about five or six stories in the eight-story building, go into a room and sit and wait. The judge comes in wearing a pink bathrobe and slippers. He's bewhiskered.

I know, you're skeptical, 3 a.m., judge in a pink bathrobe. But this is a true story, every word of it.

"Well, boy, you done run a red light. Not only that, your license ex-parred."

"Judge, I'm on active duty on my way to Vietnam. Federal law is I can drive with an expired license because I got deployed over there."

"Well, you're in Joe-jah now, boy. Fifty dollah."

Now, this was a long time ago, and 50 dollars was a lot of money. "I don't have 50 dollars, Judge."

"Well, you go 'cross the street and the bah-tindah will cash your check."

I cross the street, and the bartender takes a small rake-off for cashing my check. I cross back over, walk back up six flights, and say, "Judge, I'm feeling a bit sandbagged. I think I'd like my day in court."

"Not a problem, boy. You wait in that cell, and the judge'll be through here on the 16th of January." (Remember, it's the 20th of December.) What's he talking about? A special judge for speed-trap victims?

I gave him the 50 dollars. And vowed I'd get even somehow.

CHAPTER TWENTY-ONE
Welcome to Southeast Asia

When I got to Vietnam in early January, 1965, my job was flying the "mail run," delivering supplies around the country. On my off time, I "worked" the bars in Saigon. Now a pig with false eyelashes and a ribbon on its tail is still a pig, but one of the C-47s has more than ribbons. Three Gatling guns stick out its side. It's called the FC-47. I volunteer for every damned one of the FC's flights, even though I'm just the co-pilot, figuring with a little luck I might get a swap. I'm also looking long term, reckoning I'd do a year in Vietnam flying C-47s then get a decent assignment going back to the States.

Well, I get promoted to the left seat. Now I'm the pilot, not the co-pilot. Three Gatling guns sticking out the side. There's no gunsight or anything. You just put a grease mark on the pilot's side window and lean over and shoot up VC campfires. That was all right, but we couldn't get permission from headquarters when we got a real target to shoot at. I remember one night flying the FC-47, I see all these big transport ships unloading in a no-go zone, a restricted area up near Nha Trang. Clearly unloading supplies for the Viet Cong. I ask for permission to shoot up the ships. "Oh no, we can't do that."

Then, in March of '65, I'm flying the Saigon R and R run out of Bien Hoa, and the squadron commander of all the aircraft in the 1st Air Commandos—all the planes except the A-1s—takes the right seat, the co-pilot's seat, to sort of get to know me and assess my performance.

On the way back, he looks over at me and says,

"You oughta be flying fighters."

Ha-hah. Remember that everything good that has ever happened to me is because of other people doing stuff for me.

"You oughta be flying fighters. I'll speak to the wing commander."

The next thing I know, they're giving me an in-theater checkout in the A-1E, the only such checkout they ever gave. Even though the A-1 (a Korean war era prop fighter) wasn't what I would have liked to be flying, it was the only fighter the US was using in Southeast Asia at the time, in accordance with the Geneva Convention. (We weren't "combatants" at the time, just "trainers" or whatever the hell they decided to call us.)

We didn't have jets in theater yet. They didn't come in until spring of '65, and this was just before that. When the French got kicked out of Indochina in the '50s, the Geneva Accords separated Vietnam into North Vietnam (communist) and South Vietnam, headed by the former emperor. The Americans were not party to the Accords, but we adhered to the rules, and one of the covenants was there would be no jet aircraft in the theater, ever.

So we had to fly these A1-Es, old Korean Air Force prop fighters, and actually they were a lot of fun. Of course, it was a war, but you wouldn't have known it in the south. When our Army finally came in, we flew close air support for them. That was legitimate war, and we got shot at, but before that, it was mostly going out and dropping bombs on trails and rice paddies and shooting up buffalo, VC pack animals, and an occasional truck.

It was an early part of the war. We had no clue that it would evolve into something so big, something so serious, so deadly. When I look back, I think, "Well, my part was small." I'm glad it wasn't much bigger, but it still hurts looking back on all the guys we lost, and for what?

A few weeks after I started flying the A-1Es, the US government said the hell with the Geneva Accords, and we sent the F-100s north, on which mission we lost Hayden Lockhart, the second American pilot shot down in North Vietnam. Hayden was a classmate of mine both at the Air Force Academy and at pilot training. A great guy. He was shot down on 2 March 1965 and held as a POW until 2 February 1973. Almost eight years!

CHAPTER TWENTY-TWO
Depth Perception vs. Flying

Okay, I told you about my forgettable baseball career and my discovery that I had no depth perception. Apparently, I never had any, but in the Air Force, this deficiency complicated my life a bit, because of how it affected my landings. Compensation for no depth perception on a bright day is easy. You have shadows and relative sizes of objects near each other and so forth. Night landings are a different matter, and I occasionally dropped them in pretty hard, but nothing too serious. Until one day in Vietnam.

I'm in my A-1E, flying low over a canal, a little too low, maybe, strafing Viet Cong sampans. Each of my 20-millimeter high explosive bullets is like a mini grenade. A lot of the mud in the bank comes shooting up into the sky about 50 feet. Unfortunately, I'm a bit lower than that and the mud splatters all over my windshield and the engine and everything else.

Back at altitude, I call the rest of the flight. "I'll be a little late getting in, go on back without me." In my right seat is Jim Ahmann, an Academy classmate who I'm taking along for the ride. I have a brilliant plan to clean the mud off the windshield. I ask Jim to get his canteen out and wet his "overseas" cap (the cloth folding blue uniform cap universally referred to by an anatomical body part which cannot be printed here), carried in a flight-suit pocket. Then I ask him to unstrap, stand up in the seat, open the canopy, and clean off the windshield. I throttle back to about 120 knots. Jim does as instructed, and next thing, he's hanging on for dear life, damn near getting sucked out of the airplane!

When I get back, to base, I can't see a damned thing out of the windshield. I open my side canopy, lean out and try to judge my height by looking directly down at the runway. Normally, it would be a tough job. Without depth perception, well, I drop the plane in from 35 feet and blow all three tires. Can't taxi. Have to get towed in. Beyond embarrassing.

Jim Ahmann, who was almost sucked out of my plane, is an FAC, (forward air controller), a dangerous and heroic job in combat zones, but I have managed to scare the crap out of him, drive his hemorrhoids right up to his tonsils, and, quite possibly, send him straight back to the jungle for rest and recuperation.

I'm raw meat for any brass who sees that airplane. But my crew chief is another great guy. Upon seeing my crippled, muddy, once lovely Douglas Skyraider, he says, "Jesus Christ, Brice, what did you do?" Without waiting for an answer, he turns to his guys and says, "Get this airplane in the hangar right now, and close the doors." Which they do, and I escape another bullet.

Interesting fact: In our day, we had to be fully medically qualified to get to the Academy, and lack of depth perception was an instant disqualification for pilot training. When I took the physical to get into the Academy, that's the only depth perception test I ever passed. They either missed it or flubbed their own job. For whatever reason, once again, things just happened.

After that, every time I had to take a physical, the examiner would say, "You've gotten this far, I'm not going to flunk you out." I got all the way through pilot training and years of flying the line before some medic in Vietnam said, "You've got no depth perception. You're grounded." By then I'd been flying let's say five years, and I was ungrounded within 36 hours, because I was already a qualified pilot, and all I had to do was get a pair of corrective glasses, which, of course, I never wore.

CHAPTER TWENTY-THREE
Big George

So, I finish up '65 as an A-1 pilot. My hoochmate is Will Cannon, a ground pounder assigned to intelligence. We get along famously and tie one on once or twice, or more. A month or two after I start flying A- 1s, Brigadier General "Big George" Simler, Southeast Asia Air Ops Officer, puts out the word he's looking for an aide-de-camp. In theory he isn't allowed an aide-de-camp, but in practice all the top brass have them. The aide has to be a non-rated guy (no pilots), Will is a super competent West Point grad, and he gets the job. And Big George loves him.

Now it's December, the end of Will's year in Vietnam, and the end of my year as well. Will gets reassigned stateside, and Big George says, "I've gotta have a replacement for you."

As I said, there's always a guy who's there for me at the right time and place. Will, that guy, says, "Why don't you get Brice Jones? Great guy."

Everybody calls General Simler "Big George," except to his face. I go down to Saigon and have dinner with Will and Big George, who is damned big, all muscle, and an F-105 fighter pilot. He'd commanded a wing of them, around 80 pilots, in Okinawa, and now he is in charge of all tactical air ops in Southeast Asia. Big George says, "The job's yours if you want it. Do you mind staying here another year?"

Do I *want* it? Do I *mind*? I'm a *career* officer. You couldn't write a better position for a career officer in my boots. Aide to General Big George Simler, man's man, fighter pilot's fighter pilot, with the number one job in the air war! Not just yes, HELL YES!

So I move in and become his aide-de-camp, still maintaining my combat certification in the A-1. But, officially, he can't call me his "aide-de-camp," so he gives me another title: "You are the Combat Tactics Officer for A-1s."

That's a hell of a title because it sounds so impressive. When I went back to the Academy for an award a few years ago, they asked me to write a little resumé and I put that title down. And Bob Brickey, my Academy classmate, All-American football player, godfather of my firstborn, called me up and said, "What school did you go to to get Combat Tactics?"

Oh well, busted, I suppose. Then again, it was Big George who anointed me with that job title. I mean, it's a bit like telling Babe Ruth he's not the Sultan of Swat, when some writer invented that title just for him.

CHAPTER TWENTY-FOUR

Vietnam Reflections

When I got to Vietnam in early '65, it was still a kind of blue-ribbon volunteer thing for the military, at least for the Air Force. I was a career officer, gung-ho, wanted to do everything right, respected authority, more or less. When the President said, "Go to war," we went to war. And I did my duty flying A-1s, Korean war-era prop fighters. In 1954, the Viet Minh under Ho Chi Minh defeated the French at the Battle of Dien Bien Phu. The subsequent Geneva Accord included a prohibition of jet aircraft in Vietnam. Hence my A-1E prop fighter.

We were being called upon to interdict supplies being sent south from North Vietnam, and a lot of our interdiction involved shooting up VC pack animals, that is to say, water buffalo. Other typical targets were structures, even in small villages. We were told the inhabitants were harboring the VC, and our actions would prompt the villagers to get those guys out of there. As my first year moved along, in my first few months it just didn't seem much like a war to me. I got shot at and dropped a lot of bombs and stuff, but it didn't seem like a war, and it didn't seem like we were getting anywhere. Then came the "build-up." Up till then, the US Army had been acting in an advisory capacity to the Vietnamese Army. But, to be honest, the Vietnam soldiers just weren't interested. They'd been at war their entire lives and didn't need more. So in the spring of '65, "Washington" decided we'd take it on ourselves. The "Domino Theory," don't you know? One country goes commie, then the next, then the next, till there are little hammers and sickles instead of stars on Old Glory.

LBJ had just been elected and was intent on pushing his "Great Society" program through Congress. He couldn't take the distraction of negative press, so, no matter how things in Vietnam progressed, we were "winning."

Jets arrived, most stationed in Thailand, and they started bombing bridges and roads in North Vietnam. The A-1 mission became primarily close-air support for the US Army. At least we were doing some good for our own guys. That mission continued for me until my one-year tour of duty was just about complete, and I was invited to have dinner in Saigon with Big George.

Working for Big George was an education. He was a natural leader, and I "watched and learned." He was also a professional and brooked no nonsense or wasted effort. But, like all the generals, he was in it for the longer haul and more stars on his shoulders. He already had one star for this job, and he, like all the rest, wanted four. So he was great for what he could control. But there was an endless amount of pure horse crap emanating from Washington: targeting, micro-management, directives from LBJ and his whizz kids, visits by McNamara. And Big George, like them all, was the good soldier.

I watched General Westmoreland, Commander, United States Military Assistance Command, Vietnam, before he became Chief of Staff of the entire US Army, make some decisions that I thought were awful. Generals strutted around headquarters bragging about the war. One day, an Army general, I won't mention his name, was walking around the 7th Air Division headquarters bragging about a battle that his troops had been in that week. They had lost 167 men. And he was bragging about losing those men! Reveling in the fact it must have been a hell of a battle to lose 167 guys. He was just as proud as he could be that he lost 167 American soldiers.

I thought I would throw up.

Though I was Big George's aide, I still flew occasional missions both to keep my flight status current and to be able to report to Big George on things that were *really* going on in the field. One night we went out to Laos on an interdiction on a trail. I was riding in the right seat, observing, and we beat up some nondescript part of the trail—all I saw were trees. We completed the bombing, in accordance with directions from the forward air controller (FAC) who was flying in a small egg-beater plane down in the trees, as it were. We were leaving the target area, when he came on the horn and said, "I'm giving you guys 75 trucks destroyed and 50 KBA," (50 enemy combatants killed by air). I was beside myself. I didn't see one truck, and I don't know how he could decide that we killed anybody by air, but that was what the war was becoming: a ginning up of so-called battle statistics.

Westmoreland got sued later on after the war by somebody who said, "You're manufacturing statistics." The suit was settled out of court, but the guy who sued him was right as rain. It wasn't that Westmoreland sent down orders, "Make up statistics." It's just that the ethos became, "We've got to have a lot of big numbers."

Our own military (at least at the leadership level), was our biggest enemy in Vietnam. The main battle the Air Force fought, day after day, was against the Navy. The Navy would come in with statistics, and we'd have to get statistics to beat them. I attended those briefings all the time. The Navy would figure out a way to get credit for more targets hit, or number of missions than the Air Force, and we'd have to beat that. So the bogus info contest between the Air Force and the Navy was our biggest battle.

McNamara would come over, get briefed by the generals, and go back and espouse an embellished company line. But the generals, in my observation, were not really all-in for the fighting man. I was in a briefing for Westmoreland at one point, and one of his guys said, "We've been ordered to do blah, blah, and blah." And Westmoreland discussed it a little bit and wanted to know if he had the authority to move an aircraft carrier. He didn't even know what his authority included and didn't want to take a chance on exceeding it. In another instance, I saw him acquiesce to a Washington directive, even though he knew it was not the best solution for the troops fighting the battle. I thought he should have spoken up and said, "We're not going to do that. We're going to do what's right," and, since he was countermanding a directive from Washington, he should have stood up from that table, ripped his stars off, thrown them on the table and said, "Get another lackey to do it." But of course, he didn't. And that's the reason that H.R. McMaster wrote in his book *Dereliction of Duty* that the senior commanders resembled the three monkeys who "hear no evil, see no evil, speak no evil." The generals were all just preserving their careers.

CHAPTER TWENTY-FIVE
The Wine Bug

Now it's 1966, an auspicious year for American wine. Robert Mondavi "invents" premium wine in America with the introduction of stainless steel, refrigeration, and hygiene. Before that it was all Paul Masson, Almaden. We did have Mountain Chablis, but it was just plonk.

The same year, 1966, I get bitten by the wine bug. While Mondavi's opening up a new era in American wine, I'm in Vietnam, aide-de-camp for Brigadier General George Simler. Turns out Simler considers himself a wine buff. On later reflection, I figure that probably was because he was shot down in France in World War II and had an underground resistance guy, Pierre, who was assigned to get him out to Switzerland. I can just see them sneaking through moonlit vineyards, stopping at farmhouses, drinking wine. Big George named his first- born Pierre. I don't blame him. Pierre saved his ass and introduced him to French wine.

One day over lunch Big George says to me, "You know Captain, Burgundy is the name of a place."

"Aww General, you're pulling my leg. Burgundy is a brand of Paul Masson. Even I know that."

"Nope. Look it up."

Well, we don't have gadgets to look things up in those days, nor do we have a non-military library in Vietnam, so I wait until

I get back to the States. Eventually, I look up "Burgundy" and, what do you know, Burgundy is a place!

I start going to retail stores, looking at French wine labels, trying different wines, appreciating the better ones. And before you know it, I'm hooked.

Chapter Twenty-Six
Naming Monte

A while ago, I was in one of my local haunts with my son Monte. An acquaintance asked how my son got that name, and I realized that there was more about Monte Moorberg I wanted to tell.

We roomed together for two years at the Academy, sophomore and senior years. Monte and I were close. He was a strong cadet, strong physically and strong mentally. He was a pretty good student and a superb football player, fullback. He scored the very first touchdown ever for AF against Army. His father Earl got a job on the construction of the Academy, and the whole family moved to Colorado Springs to watch Monte play football. I spent a fair amount of time over at his house. Earl Moorberg was the salt of the earth. Monte's mother worked selling tickets at a Colorado Springs movie theater. Earl was a down-to-earth Grand Island, Nebraska laborer. He was such a nice, good guy. And his son was the same.

In senior year, Monte broke his wrist in summer football drills. He shouldn't have played football that senior year with his hand and wrist in a cast, but the coach talked him into it, telling him, Monte, play with that broken wrist, and I'll make sure you get into pilot training when you graduate. Well, Monte played football and he graduated, but because of the wrist, he didn't pass the physical for flight school. He was a rated navigator, as we all were, a course we took at the Academy, so off he went to navigate something big that flew around and around. Not a happy time for him.

After six months, he did get into flight training. I don't know if the coach had anything to do with it, but Monte got accepted into a training class at the same base where Brusk and I were—Webb AFB in Big Spring, Texas. Months after me, he graduated from flight school and was assigned to F-102s, interceptors, for the Air Defense Command.

I remember when his number came up for Vietnam. They checked him out in F-105 fighter-bombers, and Monte told me he didn't want to go. I think he had a premonition. Even all these years later I choke up when I think about it. When they eventually had his funeral, I gave the eulogy, and I said I could imagine his last night at home, the way he was putting his kids to bed, hugging them and kissing them. I think he knew he wasn't coming back. But Monte was strong, honorable and patriotic, and he went.

I'll never forget that call in the night in 1966. I had returned from Vietnam and was in Phoenix. Monte's wife Judy was on the line. "Monte is missing."

I called Monte's command post in Vietnam and found out what had happened. Monte was flight lead, flying in Route Pack VI over and around Hanoi, the most dangerous target sector in North Vietnam. He was hit. His wingman radioed, you're burning, and your plane is coming apart. Get out of there. But he wouldn't get out. Should have headed straight for the ocean and bailed out. But the protocol was to wait till all the planes in the flight got back together, and then go home as an integral unit. He was on fire. He should have pulled the handles (ejected) then and there. He didn't. He circled until all four guys had made their passes, and they all headed back to Thailand together. But by then flames were consuming him in the cockpit and there was nothing left to fly. His squadron commander, Neil Eddins, who later commanded the Thunderbirds, told me they loved Monte in his squadron and called him one of the "young horses." I understand that entirely.

Monte had told me he never wanted to be taken prisoner. So he didn't bail out, till finally it was either pull the handles or be cremated alive. He ejected, but his chute apparently never opened. He hit the ground at probably 100mph, and that was that.

They hypothesized that the flames in the cockpit melted the parachute harness, which was polyester or nylon or some sort of plastic, and of course the risers were nylon, so the chute couldn't deploy properly. He had a streamer. Everyone knew he was gone. But the Air Force didn't declare him dead. They didn't have the body, and it's financially better for the widow if you're still listed as on active duty, but missing in action, because once you're declared dead, your benefits evaporate. So they kept Monte MIA for a couple of years. Unfortunately, in many cases, like this one, the policy can give false hope to the survivors. Consequently, I made sure the family all knew he was lost, so that when that blue AF staff car with the chaplain in it pulled up to Judy's house, she didn't fall down in a faint.

When his bones finally came home in '82, a dozen classmates and I met the plane at Andrews AFB, Washington DC, and we went with the casket to Arlington National Cemetery, where he was buried.

His father thought Lash Larue, the old-time movie cowboy, was a pretty good character to name his son after, so his full name was Monte Larue Moorberg. My friend; my brother...

We didn't know if my second son was going to be a boy or a girl before he was born, but I told Susan that, boy or girl, the baby should be named Monte. And she agreed. I never wanted to tell my son Monte how he got named because I didn't want him to feel any strange karma about it. But it's interesting that while he had his choice of Academies to attend, my Monte didn't want to go to the Air Force Academy—even though he was willing to fly by the time he went to West Point. When he graduated, he wanted to go to the Marines, but the Marine Corps wouldn't take him because he had no history of Marines in the family. I sat on a charitable board with the past Commandant of the Marine Corps, the celebrated P.X. Kelley, a four-star general. I had supported the cause generously, and I figured it would be a slam-dunk to get General Kelley to take Monte into The Corps. During a break in a board meeting at an opportune moment, I raised the subject, but he just responded dead-panned with the HQ position: "Sorry, no history of Marines in your family. That's just the way it is."

So Monte went Armor (tanks) and served his five years, including a year in Iraq. When he put in his resignation at the end of his tour, the higher-ups tried mightily to keep him with hot-shot offers of big jobs, but he was ready to move on. A couple years later he did the MBA program at Darden School of Business, UVA and went to work with his brother Victor. Today, they produce maybe the best ciders in America, made from fresh fruit, not Chinese concentrate. They get gold medal after gold medal, "Best in Show," after "Best in Show." They do it all virtually by themselves, the two of them and a laborer. I couldn't be prouder of both of them.

If you want to give their delicious ciders a try, send Victor a shout at *victor@missiontrailranches.com.*

Victor and Monte Jones at Mission Trail Ranch.

CHAPTER TWENTY-SEVEN

Choice of Assignments

When Big George Simler took me on as his aide-de-camp, he said, "I want you to be my eyes and ears in the field." So I'd fly a few fighter missions, go to different bases, surreptitiously inspect them, and write reports for Simler. After reading my reports, Big George would call people into his office and say, "Base Commander, it has come to my attention that your base *growl-growl-growl* and *blah-blah-blah.*" And he'd rip him a new one while I'm sitting in the back trying to hide my eyes.

Most noons, Simler wanted to play tennis, so I went to the officer in charge of the tennis courts and reserved a court for us for every day at noon. One day, there were four majors playing on Big George's court. I went over to them and said that we had that court. Big George was standing back, in his shorts, tennis racket tucked under his arm, letting his aide do the talking. And the majors said they weren't moving.

Big George went ballistic. He threw his racket over the court, over the fence and onto the roof of a two-story building on the other side.

Rattle bang clang! The roof was metal. The building occupants poured out, looking for cover. Remember, this was Vietnam, and bad things were happening. The majors wisely disappeared.

I remember a guy who was unhappy working in the planning shed at headquarters for Simler. He was an F-105 pilot, and he kept bugging the general about going back to flying the line (combat). And Big George would tell him to go back to his office and do his job. One day, Simler and I went out to the flight line to get on a T-39 for an inspection trip to somewhere, and there was the disgruntled 105 pilot, standing in front of the ladder, and he wouldn't move.

Simler barks, "Move!"

The guy stands there. "I'm not moving till you let me go back to 105s."

"You'll get an assignment, all right. Back to the States for your court martial! Move!"

Guy moves. I'm surprised he had enough guts to even try what he did, but later, when I wanted F-105s in Vietnam, I kind of understood.

Big George could be a wild man. When I came back to the States and eventually got out of the AF a few years later, I drove from California to Harvard, and I stopped in San Antonio to see him. At that time, he was the commander of Air Training Command. He had five children, one a beautiful girl several years younger than I was. (Big George thought I was a good son-in-law prospect). I got to his house about 2 o'clock in the afternoon. The general was at work, and his wife said, "I don't know if you want to see him right now. Yesterday, he came home from playing golf, and last night around midnight, he made Mike (his youngest son, who was about 12) put on all his scuba gear, and he took him to the golf course to get his clubs out of the lake."

Dark ops, right? He had that kind of temper.

83

He was a real fighter pilot, great guy, 105 pilot. The day he pinned on his fourth star, he took a T-38 to go to his next duty station, attempted a roll on takeoff but dished out too low and "bought the farm."

Anyway, after my year in Vietnam with him, Simler gave me my choice of assignments: I said, "I want F-104s at George AFB." So that's what I got. But about a month before I'm due to go, I say, "You know, General, I've been thinking. If I check in as an A1 pilot at George, they're going to think I'm just an old propeller pilot, not really a jet fighter pilot, and they're going to—"

"So, you want to go to Luke (AFB in Phoenix) first?"

"Yes, sir, I want to go to Luke first and check out in F-100s, and then go to George Air Force Base for F-104s."

So Big George pulls strings, and I get sent to Luke. But while I'm there, checking out in the F-100, the Air Force starts phasing the 104 out. It was a rocket, fast, high altitude, but it really wasn't a good weapons platform, too small. So the Pentagon calls:

"Well, Captain Jones, what do you want to do now?"

"I want to go back to Southeast Asia in 105s."

The Pentagon guy says, "We're not giving you that. We'll give you any other assignment in the Air Force, but not 105s in Southeast Asia. You can have attaché in London, South America, F-4s in Tucson."

"I want 105s in Southeast Asia."

He wouldn't give it to me. I call Simler, and he says, "I tried, but I can't get it for you."

Ever since then, I've heard people say stuff like, "Oh, I work at Hewlett Packard, and they won't do this or that." Or, "Oh, I work for the phone company, and they don't allow that."

It's not HP. It's not the phone company. It's some guy! It's some (bleep) sitting behind a desk. In the Air Force, the guy is usually a major.

Even General Simler can't get 105s for me. So I figure out who this guy in the Pentagon is, and I go to see him. There he sits, behind his desk. I want to turn it right over on him. I say, "Why won't you give me that 105?"

"Because you've had too much of what you want, and that's not the way the Air Force works."

The way the Air Force works? He won't give me 105s because that's what I want! Of course, the guy is right on both counts, but still, I'm not asking for attaché in London or such. I'm not asking for a cushy job. I'm asking for the hairiest job in the Air Force, flying F-105s in Vietnam.

Statistics were if you flew a 105 for the assigned 100 missions in the North, you had a 67% chance of not completing those 100 missions—that is being shot down. Of the 67% shoot-downs, half were extracted, that is rescued, and half were either killed or went to the Hanoi Hilton. But I wanted to do it. I was a career officer, I had all the right check marks on my resume, and, in my own mind, I was on my way to becoming a two or three-star general. (At the time, of course, I was only a captain.)

I told this guy in the Pentagon that I wanted to fly 105s, and he said nope, we'll give you any other assignment in the Air Force, but not that one.

A few years ago, I played a round of golf with an Academy classmate. He had stayed in the Air Force, retired with two stars on his shoulders, and never once questioned his assignment. Flew C-124s, aka "Old Shakey," for eons, because that was his assignment. I couldn't have done that. Just couldn't.

Brice and his F-100.

So after being told what I can't do, I'm still an F-100 pilot assigned to Myrtle Beach. Where is the action? Where is the place I want to be? Certainly not in Myrtle Beach. I'm still a career officer. I still want an honorable career. I just don't want to waste my time. So I decide to go to grad school on the Air Force's dime.

Two classmates at the Academy, Art Kerr and Phil Woods, had gone to graduate business schools and one more, Sam Hardage, was en route at that time, (turned out they all went to Harvard). But I didn't know anything about grad schools, certainly nothing about business schools. I didn't even know Harvard *had* a business school. I grew up in the military. Anyway, I applied with the Air Force to go to grad school in business. Figured it might rescue my career.

In late '67, when the Air Force declared Monte officially dead, his widow Judy asked me to come up to Grand Island to participate in his memorial service. I appropriated a T-33, and off I went. After the service, I'm kicking the tires before my flight back to Myrtle Beach, and a guy in his blues comes striding across the ramp straight at me. About 30 feet away he yells, "Don't you recognize a friend, Jones?" It's Mike Carnes, Class of '59. I know him because he was a hell of a handball player, and I was pretty good, so we played each other in intramural tournaments. Eventually, he became a four-star general and Vice Chief of Staff. At this point, he was a major, and I was a captain.

Mike asked, "What are you doing with your career?"

I said, "I struck out at going back to Southeast Asia, so I'm requesting the AF send me to grad school."

"In what?"

"Business."

"Where?"

"I think I'd like to go to Georgetown."

"Georgetown?" (Unbeknownst to me, Mike had just graduated from Harvard Business School.) "There's only one business school. Harvard."

I said, "Harvard has a business school?"

"Yeah. You fly back home. I'll take care of this."

I flew back to Myrtle Beach, and by then I'm such a *persona non grata* with the Air Force they send me temporary duty for 6 months to Korea, because the USS Pueblo, our Navy "spy" ship, was attacked and seized by North Korea. Part of the U.S. response was sending a half dozen fighter pilots without planes to Osan, where we growled across the border at the North Koreans. *Grrrrr!* Six fighter pilots without airplanes.

So, anyway, they sent me to Osan to growl and play ping pong. At Mike Carns's urging I had sent an application to Harvard Business School. One day, in Korea, the phone rang. "This is the Dean of Admissions at Harvard. Mr. Jones, you will have to take the BSAT (Business Scholastic Aptitude Test) if you want to come here."

To me it didn't matter a lot whether I went to Harvard or not, so I said, "I'm in Korea. I can't do that." He said, "You have to take the BSAT."

I checked with the officer in charge of the six of us, and he okayed it. I got Space A (Space Available) to Guam, to Wake, to Johnson, to Hawaii, to San Francisco, and five days after leaving Korea I was in Atlanta, Georgia. Got off the plane at 6 a.m., took a cab straight to some auditorium and took the BSAT in my flight suit. At the end of the day, I went back to the airfield and headed back to Korea. Five more days of Space Available.

When my stint in Korea was over, I went back to Myrtle Beach, not knowing if I would be accepted at Harvard. But I had taken the BSAT.

Then the "Air Force" (by now you know who this really was: a dork sitting at a desk in Ohio), informed me they were sending me to USC (Southern Cal), in computers. I didn't know if Harvard was going to accept me, but I said there was no way I was going to USC in computers, and they said, oh yes you are. So I sort of stole an airplane, flew up to Wright Patterson AFB in Ohio, and found the guy who made the decision. I found the guy!

I barged into his office. "What the hell are you doing to me? I am not going to Southern Cal!"

"Why not?"

"Because I don't want to sit in a windowless room in Oklahoma City for the rest of my career."

"Well, that's where you're going."

"No, I'm going to Harvard." I really didn't know this, but I was a pretty decent poker player.

"Oh, you'll never get in there. Your grades are no good, and your BSAT stinks. You'll never get into Harvard."

"Call 'em."

So he picked up the phone: "I'm calling about Brice Jones, Brice C. Jones. He applied for—Really?" He hangs up. "I'll be damned. They're letting you in."

I said, "Then I'm going, right?"

"No. You're going to Southern Cal in computers."

"You've gotta be kidding me."

He wasn't kidding. He said, "Why be so stupid? All you have to do is lie on the beach, drink beer, ogle all the honeys, and in 18 months you're an MBA. What's wrong with you?"

"Nothing. Just want Harvard B school, where I've been accepted."

"Well, that's not where you're going."

Sound familiar?

I went back to Myrtle and turned in my resignation from the AF. But they wouldn't let me out. For two years I fought it. Finally got the aide to the Chairman of the House Armed Services Committee to take up my cause. That worked, and I was out in March 1970.

In the meantime, I was flying F-100s for a year. Then my job was flying T-33s, training bomber pilots to be FACs (forward air controllers), and Egyptians to fly (period). It was just awful, but everybody at Myrtle accepted it because T-birds (T-33s) were being phased out and replaced by the new A-7s. But I didn't want to fly A-7s, either. They were almost straight-wings, *subsonic*, with no afterburners. Why would I want to fly them?

I kept trying to get out, and they kept turning me down. A regular officer (which I was) as opposed to a reservist (which I wasn't) serves "at the pleasure of the president." Well, I knew it wasn't the president. It was some guy—a major, of course—behind a desk, and he wouldn't let me out!

It wasn't till after I finally did get out that my father told me that the guy in charge of the personnel office at the Pentagon was a West Point classmate of his. Dad said, "Brice, they just didn't think you really wanted to get out." Well, they were half right. I really did want to be a career officer. Remember, I was a third generation Academy career officer. The head of Personnel just didn't know or care about the crap I was otherwise being dealt. Senior officers always try to keep the younger guys on board.

When I finally got to Harvard B School, I saw the spread of the BSAT scores. I was in the bottom 11 percent of the class.

CHAPTER TWENTY-EIGHT

Hide Under a Rock

While I was at Myrtle Beach, headquarters would come down every few weeks and say, "Somebody please take an airplane and get 20 hours on it."

What the hell? I'm just doing time. They're giving me the keys to an F-100 and telling me just put 20 hours on her, son.

So off I'd go in my own private single seat jet for a week of flying and fun. This particular time they gave me an "F" model, an F-100F, which has two seats in tandem and is used for training. So, I invite the base dentist, my good friend Art Wein. Suited him up, strapped him into the back seat, and off we went, heading west. Stopped at a couple of cities and landed Thursday at Luke Air Force Base in Phoenix. Well, on final approach, the engine burped, something went out on it, and it was gonna take a day or so to fix it. Art decided to go home, so I've got some time on my hands. I decided to take a flight to LA and visit Wade Davis, my prep school classmate. Wade had gone to Harvard Business School and, at this point, I had been accepted there. Even though the Air Force wasn't going to send me, I reckoned I was somehow going to go on my own.

I went to see Wade because I wanted to find out what I could read to get a head start. I didn't have a clue about civilian schools in general and Harvard in particular, and I was a little apprehensive about it. Wade was a portfolio investment manager at that time, and I considered him a pretty big wheel. I went into his office, and it was the same old Wade, but with long black hair almost to his shoulders. I asked him which books I should read to get a head start at Harvard.

"Books?" He laughed. "Harvard doesn't use books. It's all case study."

"What do you mean they don't use books?" Good God, I was stunned.

Long story short, I changed the subject. "I've got a jet fighter in Phoenix with two seats in it, an F-100. How'd you like to fly with me? We can fly commercial back to Phoenix, and tomorrow morning my plane will be gassed and ready. We'll take her up—you'll have a blast."

He laughed again. "I'd love to, but I'm getting married on Sunday, and tomorrow is my rehearsal dinner."

"Well, congratulations on the wedding. Tell your bride I wish both of you well."

"No, wait!" he said. "I can still squeeze this in. I'm gonna go."

Okay. We took Continental Airlines back to Phoenix that afternoon and went to the home of a pilot friend, Alex McDermott, and party, party, partied. The next morning, Alex drove us out to the flight line. Remember, Wade's got long, black hair—well, long compared to standard military officer/pilot white-sidewall length. McDermott lent him a flight suit. We went out to the ramp, and I took him into the parachute room. Got him outfitted with a parachute, helmet, oxygen mask, and "g-suit" and we went out to the plane. He carried his rehearsal suit in a zippered suit bag. Of course, it was a Brooks Brothers $400 suit. Huge money in 1968. He intended to change when we got off the plane in Albuquerque, the closest I could get him to LA, then go down to Continental Airlines, get on a flight back to LA, and go straight to the church for the rehearsal and then to the dinner.

Now, an F-100 doesn't have a suitcase pod or anything like that. I folded up his bag and stuffed it in the gun bay. To access it, you pull a door off at the nose. There are four cannons up there, two on each side. I stuffed the suit bag in and put the door back on. Between the door and the airplane there's an intake to get circulating air through to blow out the smoke from the guns, and then there's an exhaust port so air circulates all the way through the gun bay.

Parachute guys, oxygen guys, crew chiefs, the guys strapping him into the airplane all looked at Wade's long hair with puzzled faces. I told them he was a civilian doctor with NASA. We strapped him in, and I told him, "Here's all you need to know: See these two yellow handles, one on each side of the seat? You pull those up and you eject just a millisecond ahead of me. I'll be right behind you. The handles blow the canopy off and fire your rocket seat, and remember this, Wade: If we do punch out, when we get on the ground, a chopper will come to pick me up. You can't let them see you. Hide under a rock or something. I'll be back to get you eventually but, you're not getting on that chopper. I am, but you're not."

Having explained all this, I took off and headed for the Grand Canyon. I got through Mach One so he'd have bragging rights. Not many civilians had busted the "sound barrier" in those days. Then I dipped down into the Canyon, going north to south at 400–450 knots. Pulling up out of the Canyon at about 450 knots, instinctively, for some reason, I turned the airplane up on its right wing, 90 degrees. At that instant, a flash of blue streaked by on my left. We're belly to belly. He's rolled up on a wing too. It's a Navy guy going into the Canyon in the opposite direction.

We missed each other by no more than 15 or 20 feet, each of us going something like 450 or so. We would have been just vaporized had we not missed each other.

We got to Albuquerque, I parked, opened up the canopy, and Wade tossed out two barf bags right onto the ramp. The sergeant in charge of the airplane dodged them. "What the hell?"

"He's with NASA," I explained. "He's a doctor with NASA. Doesn't really fly much."

In those days we could order up a staff car, and I had done that. The staff car took us over to the BOQ overnight visitors' quarters. Wade showered, took his first look at his suit bag, and there's a hole the size of a volleyball, well maybe a softball, clear through the bag and his suit coat. The air blowing through the gun bay had ripped right through it all.

He put on a white shirt, necktie, and the remnants of his coat. The shirt shone through the back like a big white splat. I said to myself, "Where am I gonna get 400 dollars to pay for his suit?" But Wade says, "Don't worry. I like it."

I'll never forget watching Wade Davis walk up the sidewalk to the Continental Airlines terminal with a big hole in the back of his Brooks Brothers jacket. He went to his rehearsal, proud as he could be of the "Mach One Hole."

Wade Davis, one day before tying the knot, ten minutes before takeoff, and sixty seconds before Brice tells him that if they eject he'll have to hide under a rock.

Seven or eight years later, Wade made the acquaintance of Sam Hardage, my Academy classmate. Wade had Sam over to dinner one night. During the course of the dinner, Sam mentioned that he had been in the Air Force.

Wade said, "Oh, I know an Air Force guy. I roomed with him in prep school." Without saying my name, he added, "This guy gave me a ride in an F-100."

Sam, incredulous, said, "No, you're mistaken. You're a civilian. You did not get a ride in an F-100. It was something else."

Wade said, "Oh no, it was an F-100," and he got up from the table, went into his den and brought back a picture of him decked out in his flight gear, standing in front of the F-100, and Sam said,

"Well, there is *one* guy..."

CHAPTER TWENTY-NINE
Cash Flo

Getting accepted at Harvard Business School was a little more complicated the second time around. The first time, I was supposed to be sponsored by the Air Force, and they would foot the bill. The second time, I was a civilian, paying my own way, and Harvard asked me for my parents' financial statement. I said no way (not that there would have been much to it). I'm 30 years old. I'm not going to lean on them for dough at this age. Gotta say this for Harvard, they hold themselves to a higher standard, and the fact that they had already accepted me once, with Uncle Sam in my wallet, overruled their judgment of the new civilian me, with empty pockets turned inside out. And Mike Carns, bless him, was in my corner, telling them what a leader I was. So I went to Harvard and borrowed every cent of my expenses from them.

I talk about "the guy," the person who, at different stages of my life, was instrumental in getting me where I am today. While I was at Harvard, "the guy's" name was Florence Glenn, aka "Cash Flo," the Financial Aid Officer.

I got to be pretty good friends with her. At the start of my second year, I was maxed out on the money I could borrow for the entire two years, so I went to her and said, "Miss Glenn, I'm 31 years old, I'm living in a dorm, but I just can't live at the level these young 24-year-olds do."

"Can you be specific, Mr. Jones?"

"Well, for instance, Miss Glenn, when I go on a date, I rent a Lincoln Continental and take them to Cape Cod."

"Well, Mr. Jones, we must keep up appearances."

There were a lot of "Well, Mr. Jones" occasions.

"Well, Mr. Jones, it looks as though you'll need a new wardrobe, what with all your interviews coming up. And you'll need this, and you'll need that. Do you think another five thousand will do?"

"If I'm very frugal, Miss Glenn."

At its graduation ceremony, Harvard graduates nine colleges all at once. Theology, stand up. You're graduated. Architecture, stand up. You're graduated. On and on. Ten thousand students.

After the whole thing, I had to go over to Cash Flo's office to get my diploma.

"Miss Glenn, I'm here to get my diploma."

"Well, Mr. Jones, it looks like you owe $300 in parking tickets."

"$300? I can't pay that."

"Well, then you can't have your diploma."

"Let me understand this, Miss Glenn. I have graduated?"

"Yes."

"But I can't have my diploma until I pay you 300 bucks?"

"That's right, Mr. Jones."

"You've got yourself a deal, Miss Glenn."

She kept the diploma, and I left.

I came back to pay off my loan six years early. I just loved her so much, I couldn't wait to see her. I said, "Now, Miss Glenn, the deal is: I'm paying you off six years early, but I want my diploma." We both laughed. That was a kick, and she gave me the tube with the diploma inside.

All these years later, I have no idea where that diploma is.

CHAPTER THIRTY

Business School

When I was still in business school, I spent a ton of time putting together a plan for what I thought would be an excellent tax shelter for investors: developing vineyards. I chose vineyards because Big George had piqued my interest in wine, and I realized developing vineyards could be a tax shelter because farmers were allowed cash-basis accounting. Not to bore you too much, but you could write off almost everything, even if funded by loans, so I could deliver "losses" of even 300% of the investment of equity cash. It was a pretty good deal. I put a prospectus together and took it around to most of the financial houses of the day. At that time there were lots of them. Most of them are out of business now, like Hayden, Stone, and all those guys. They all said it was too risky. Investing in government housing was safer. I just couldn't sell them on vineyards, and believe me, I spent a whole lot of time traipsing around to those places all over the country—one of the reasons I was so well acquainted with Florence Glenn.

So when I graduated, without a vineyard development deal, I took a job at Wells Fargo in San Francisco. I'm walking down Montgomery Street on a Friday in June. In three days, I'm going to start my job. There's the Wells Fargo building looming across the street. I look up at it, and a thrill of anticipation does not tickle my spine. Rather, a feeling of impending doom grabs my heart. A phone booth beckons. In case you weren't around in those ancient pre-cell phone days, a phone booth was a metal and glass container stood on end. It had a bifold glass door and room enough inside for one full-sized adult and a coin-operated telephone, a *landline*! This particular phone booth says to me, "Come in, Brice, I'm your friend in your time of need." I enter, fumble coins from my pocket, dial, and get the guy I'm supposed to work for. (He could have come to his window and waved.)

"Hello, Mr. Jackowitz, I know I'm coming to work for you Monday, for $16,000 a year (the median starting salary for business school grads then). What do you think I'll be making in five years?"

"Without a doubt, $20,000."

I said, "Well, sir, that's fair enough, but the trouble is, I'm 32 years old, and I don't have the time to climb that ladder. I'm sorry. I'm not coming."

I just knew I didn't have the time to start out with 16K and work my way up to 20 in five years. But now I don't have a wing or a prayer. I have no money. I owe Harvard 40,000 bucks. What have I done? I go back to Boston. It's early summer, right after graduation. The campus is quiet. I still have the key to my old dorm room. The place is empty. Dust motes swim in the air by the window. I become a squatter.

My future wife (unbeknown to both of us at the time), Susan Porth, who had also just graduated from the B school, lives across town, camped out with a girlfriend. I see her once or twice a week that summer. One day I'm out in the quad throwing a frisbee, and a friend—an ex-classmate—happens to walk by. Why would he be here, walking across an almost empty quad at Harvard Business School in the summer?

I tell him what I'm up to (nothing), and he says, "Why don't you go down to New York and talk to this guy, Kent Klineman? He used to practice law with my father and split off to become a tax shelter specialist."

So, with his referral, I make an appointment and go down to New York to see Mr. Kent Klineman.

"What can I do for you, Mr. Jones?"

"Mr. Klineman, I propose to come work for you for a year for free." (I don't know what I thought I was going to live on.) "I'll work for a year for free so I can learn this business."

"No, I don't want anybody working around here for free. But as long as you're here, do you know anything about how to do a vineyard deal?'"

Ever have a shocking, unexpected, electrifying moment like that, without having your finger in a light socket?

"I just happen to have a vineyard proposal right here in my briefcase."

"Leave it here for a week and come back and get it."

I came back in a week, and it had red marks all over it, arrows and instructions to do this and that.

"Take this, fix it, and bring it back to me in a week."

I go back to my dorm room, sit down with my Olivetti typewriter, fix it up, and take it back to New York the following Monday.

"Leave it here for a week and come back and get it."

All summer long, back and forth, every week or two, fix it up, take it back, fix it up.

On the 17th of September, 1972, Kent and I shook hands on the corner of 57th and Lex, in front of the tanning salon sign.

"You go to California and do the deal. I'll raise the money."

Through various ups and occasional downs, we operated on that handshake for 27 years. What an unbelievably great, gracious, nice guy.

My two years of work could have been for nothing, but my classmate came walking across the quad at Harvard Business School on a summer's day.

The right day, the right time, the right guy. Providential.

CHAPTER THIRTY-ONE

Wine Country

Y ou probably weren't born in Panama.I was.
You may not have learned to fly when you were 14 years old, taking off and landing on a lake in Alaska.

I did.

Maybe you weren't snowed in at the lake cabin you helped your dad build.

I was.

Maybe you didn't have a young friend whose name was Dick Hertz.

Maybe you and Dick didn't ski across the frozen lake, hitch a ride on a freight train, then fly in an Air Force helicopter, to rescue your stranded family.

Maybe you weren't a military brat who grew up living here, there, and everywhere.

But, chances are, if you like fine wine, you've found your way to California, maybe even to where my future lay:

Brice Cutrer Jones

Wine Country !

In September 1972, with Kent Klineman's handshake still warm, and his promise of investors' money burning a hole in my pocket, I headed out to California and found a studio apartment in Larkspur, a dozen miles north of San Francisco, for 100 bucks a month. The tenant was being evicted, and I paid him 20 bucks for all his furniture. Before you get too indignant, thinking I took advantage of the poor guy, you should know that "all the furniture" meant a mattress on the floor, a table that was a couple of boards on cinder blocks, and a chair or two rescued from a vacant lot. Another 15 dollars got me some pots, pans, knives, forks, and cracked pottery.

Before long, Susan Porth came out from Boston, and we set up housekeeping. I was looking for land—vineyard-plantable land—the very best I could find. Started looking in Napa but soon found that all the good land in Napa was gone. Good land in those days was for growing red wine grapes because the world was drinking about 3 to 1 red over white. In those days, the oldtimers didn't drink white as an aperitif. Still don't. If they wanted something to drink before dinner, it was whiskey or gin. I didn't know anyone who drank white wine back then. So I was looking for red wine land in Napa, and that meant bottomland, because the whole world 'round, farmers plant their highest value cash crop on the bottomland, which has the highest fertility soil and the most water retention.

In Europe, it was usually wheat on the valley floors. Up the sides of the hills were grapes, and above them olives. So I'm looking for bottomland, and I wanted Napa Valley, which had the warm climate to sugar up red grapes (called "black" grapes by the farmers of same). That meant Cabernet or Zinfandel, maybe Syrah. Today, I wouldn't take flat, bottomland for free if the deal was I'd have to plant it to grapes. It's just not where the best grapes grow—the *grand cru*. In Burgundy, the finest grapes, the *grand cru*, are just below the top of the mountain side, below those are the *premier cru*, and on the bottom of the slope are the *village*. Then on the very bottom of the hillside, below any slope, are the *vin ordinaire,* or the most common, *vin de pais.*

But in those days, almost all California grapes were grown by independent farmers to sell to wine producers. Maybe half of all the grapes grown in Napa and Sonoma went to Gallo and Italian Swiss Colony (ISC), and, except for sugar content (23% makes a wine of about 11.5% alcohol), quality wasn't much of an issue. Given minimum sugar, it was all about quantity. No farmers were getting paid by any metric other than weight. I remember one year I sold some Chardonnay to ISC, and as they pulled my gondola up to the crusher, the operator yelled out to somebody downstream, "Mixed whites!" I didn't sell grapes to that outfit again.

I don't recall that any wines of the time were actually labeled "Pinot Noir," so those grapes were not being planted at that time. There was a little bit planted in Mendocino County, but nobody knew what it was, and the only Pinot wine I knew of (Pedroncelli) was labeled something like "Burgundy." That was about it. Anyway, all the good red wine land—flat bottomland, with a warm climate to sugar up the Cab and Zin—was gone by 1972, so I moved my search over to Sonoma and made friends with two real estate agents. They were older guys, not used to seeing young punks looking for red wine land in an area considered too cold for red wine grapes, but they cast their doubts aside and helped me. There wasn't much over there in Sonoma either. Certainly not for Cabernet. Finally, one of these fellows, more a farmer than a real estate agent, came up with a piece of land near him. Kent sent out the money, and in December 1972, we bought our very first piece of land, a hay pasture, from a guy named Milt Sessions. It was both flat and hilly. We didn't want the hilly part, so we divided it and took the flat bottomland. It was not only flat, it flooded every year from the adjacent laguna, and it would sometimes go 15 feet under water. Sessions had a rowboat down there in the field so when it was under water, he could go out and divert tree stumps and other stuff floating in. In the '50s it had been planted in hops, so we figured grapes would do just fine. I put in an order for grapevines at Sonoma Grapevines, the local grapevine nursery. Kent sent out $100,000 as a deposit. But in order to contract for the future grapevines, I had to find out what kind of vines to plant.

So I went up to UC Davis, the reigning authority on all things viticultural, got advice, and audited courses, trying to get smarter in a hurry. I audited a course in wine tasting taught by the famous Maynard Amerine. Learned a lot. I audited a few other courses as well and talked to the instructors. Learned even more. I was devastated to discover that on the particular piece of land we had bought, we needed to plant *white* grapes. It was Sonoma County, cooler than Napa. It was bottomland, but due to the cool climate, I needed to plant white grapes. Not only that, the grapes should be *Chardonnay*. Well, I'd been selling myself as an expert in New York, but I had never heard the word Chardonnay, didn't even know what it was. I knew that white Burgundy was made out of white grapes, but I didn't know anything about what grapes it was made from. I wanted to come out of the deal with a shirt on my back, so I ordered

Chardonnay grapevines and continued to look for more land. In short order, we found three more pieces of land, all within five miles of the land we bought from Sessions.

Kent now owned a hell of a lot of land, and he gave me part ownership. In the spring, we put all the pieces together as a limited partnership and floated it to his new investors in New York.

Kent Klineman, partner from another world.

CHAPTER THIRTY-TWO
The Root Louse

Prior to the late 1800s, grapevines around the world were planted "on their own roots." That is, the *vigneron* simply took a cutting from a vine he liked, or more often, just bent a cane from it into the ground and let a new vine sprout from it, removed that and planted it—on its own roots. Then, in the second half of the 19th century, vineyards began declining from phylloxera, a venom injected into the vine by a root louse called by the same name. By 1878, most of the vineyards in France had died from the disease. The corrective action was to replant with American wild vines found on the East Coast along riverbanks. These vines were immune to the disease. Then the desired grape variety (Chardonnay, Cabernet, others) was budded (grafted) onto the American vine. The process required a fair amount of skill, and budders were in high demand. Eventually, all the vineyards in France and California were planted on these wild American rootstocks.

Phylloxera was present in certain areas but thought not to be present in all of California, so up through the 1950s, most vineyards were still planted "on their own roots." Yet, most new vineyards were budded to various commercial rootstock. The state's vineyard authority, UC Davis, developed a hybrid rootstock "resistant" to phylloxera that also produced a fulsome crop. This hybrid was called AXR1 (Americanis crossed with

Rupestris, version 1). In the end, "resistant" to phylloxera was not "immune" to phylloxera, and in the late 1980s, most of the AXRl vines succumbed to the disease.

As the planting boom got underway in California in the early 1970s, almost all new vineyards were planted to AXRl. Some ungrafted vines were planted in Monterey County and south, but those who planted them too soon wished otherwise. When the rootstock had been in the ground a year or so, it was then necessary to "bud" the scion, or grape variety, to the rootstock. Inasmuch as millions of vines were being developed, the need for budders was overwhelming. Some enterprising soul figured that the entire job, grafting scions to rootstocks, could be done in nurseries, by common laborers, on "benches" (horizontal surfaces), grown in small plastic tubes (sleeves). The process, known as "benchgrafting" seemed simple enough. Right.

Unfortunately, simple as it seemed, benchgrafting required close attention and knowledge, and when something went wrong, it could wreck hundreds of thousands of vines. Which is exactly what happened to Sonoma Grapevines. Unbeknownst to me at the time, the company was a new startup, founded by four amateurs, one of whom knew how to bud roses but not grapevines. It was a disaster, and it took all the initial depositors, of which I was one, down with them.

In March 1973, Sonoma Grapevines Nursery, where only months earlier we had put our $100,000 deposit, informed me that they wouldn't be delivering our grapevines (or our money back), because they'd had a crop failure and were going bankrupt. Making benchgrafts in the nursery was a new process, and not many people knew much about it. These guys sure didn't. I called Kent, and told him, "Bad news, we're losing the $100,000. The nursery's going bankrupt."

Kent said, "No problem at all, Brice—you pay it back." I didn't have $100,000 in Monopoly money.

I called up Sonoma Grapevines and said, "Don't put a lock on that door, I'm coming down there. I'm going to take it over and run it, and we'll make it work." So I took over as president, took an ownership position that was basically free, and began trying to figure out the benchgraft business and how to get our benchgrafts and/or money out. Of course, there were plenty of other customers who applauded because they wanted to get their grapevines out, too. So I found an experienced guy to run the agricultural part of the nursery. He knew enough about making benchgrafts that we had a fighting chance to turn things around. It wasn't easy, but by the fall of '73, about six months later, we got our grapevines out, and we planted them that winter.

By then I had bought more pieces of land, and we had two more partnerships. In '76, I had even bought 100 acres in Napa. So by the end of the '70s, we had around 750 acres of vineyards. In 1979, I sold the one in Napa, because I could see that our future lay in Sonoma County.

After all, we were Sonoma–Cutrer. So we got out of Napa and consolidated in Sonoma with about 650 acres, almost all Chardonnay.

And *voila*! In the late '70s, America discovered white wine. Cold and not too alcoholic, Chardonnay was suddenly a boom grape. Instead of the customary martinis, people could drink a glass of Chardonnay at lunch, go back to work, and still function. Bridge clubs discovered it. It hit the heights. And we were riding that crest. We were selling the right grapes from the right climate on excellent Burgundian-type land, at the right time. Sonoma had great conditions, almost like Burgundy, and the grapes were fabulous. By the end of the '70s, we had sold our grapes to maybe 25 different wineries in both Napa and Sonoma counties, and our reputation was through the roof. The partners in New York were jazzed, and they started chanting, "Let's have a winery. Let's have a winery."

By the end of the '70s, Kent agreed.

CHAPTER THIRTY-THREE

Patrons, Peons, Promises, & Porth

When I took over the nursery in the spring of '73, they had about 15,000 unsold, one-year-old Pinot Noir bench-grafts (enough to plant about 40 acres in those days). I knew by then that I needed Chardonnay, but rather than wait another year (or more) for brand new benchgrafts, the Pinot grafts at the nursery were invaluable, being one year old already. If we planted them, we'd get an extra year of growth on them before our Chardonnay benchgrafts could be ready. They were Pinot Noir, but I decided we'd just plant them anyway because I knew they would grow all right on our Sessions land.

Klineman said, "Yeah, plant *something,* because we have to have planted ground to get a disbursement from Prudential (the insurance company writing our mortgage). In fact, if you gotta plant potatoes out there, you go plant them."

So we planted that first 40 acres of Pinot, and it worked fine. We got our first crop in '74, and I pre-sold it all to Gallo. In those days, Gallo bought maybe 40% of the grapes in the North Coast under what they called the Patron System. A Gallo "grower rep" would come round, look at your grapes, and agree to take all your grapes *forever.* He'd say, "Okay, from now on, you're a Gallo guy." You'd shake hands, and that was that. You delivered *all* your grapes to Gallo, and the price would be set by Gallo *after* the harvest. Forever.

In about December, after the harvest, you'd get a check in the mail for the grapes, and that was that. Gallo was the Patron, and you were the peon, the indentured servant, farming his grapes for him. Well, I shook hands with the guy and sold him the whole 1974 crop. But those Pinot Noir vines down there in the bottomland just didn't seem to want to ripen their grapes, and I got worried.

At that time, Chateau St. Jean was starting a champagne winery, and the winemaker came over and said, "Hey, we'll take all those Pinot Noir grapes," still hanging there at the desirable low sugar, eighteen degrees sugar, "because that's what we want for our champagne."

I called the Gallo rep and said, "These grapes aren't ripening. You know, it's getting to be October, and they're not ripening. But they're just right for champagne. How about if I sell these this year to Chateau St. Jean?" And he said, "You can do anything you want." Of course, I didn't understand what that meant.

So I sold them to St. Jean, and I never sold another grape to Gallo. After you cross him on the Patron System, you're done. You're no longer a Gallo guy. But we did sell our Pinot Noir grapes for champagne for a number of years.

Well, we finally got our Chardonnay vines out of the nursery, and in the summer of '75, I sold the nursery back to the other shareholders and went about my Chardonnay business.

Susan Porth, girl of my dreams, and I got married in October of '75. At the same time, Korbel approached us about all of our grapes (about 400 producing acres of them by then). They were making champagne, and all of our grapes would have been ideal for them. So I agreed, and the owner, Adolf Heck, Sr., said, "Not only that, you should come and run this place." He wasn't thrilled at the prospect of his own 20-something son taking over the business. I agreed, but I had to cancel Susan's and my honeymoon so that I could be at Korbel for the '75 harvest and "run the place." When the grapes were ready, we took some up there, and Heck's son-in-law said, "You know, we don't really need you running this place, so that's not on the table."

I had canceled our honeymoon and didn't get to run Korbel either. Never sold them any more grapes after that. Maybe a bit of Gallo rubbed off on me.

But I did stay married for quite a while to dear Susan Porth.

CHAPTER THIRTY-FOUR

Combat Boots

Susan and I met at Harvard Business School where we were in the same class. The first time I saw her she was stomping across the quad. I say stomping because she was wearing Korean-era combat boots and Army fatigues. Whoa! Who is this antithesis of the blonde bouffants of my fighter pilot days? I found myself caught in her wake, drawn across the quad, and into her classroom. It was a Marketing Research class. At Harvard, you could audit a class for a few days to see if it was for you. Well, the class was okay, but the girl was sensational. I signed up for the class, and then she wasn't there anymore! I was stuck in Marketing Research for a whole semester, with my inadvertent recruiter nowhere in sight! Found out she was dating somebody else, but I never gave up on her. The whole first year at Harvard, I dated other girls, but Susan Porth still had a hold on me. She was everything I'd ever dreamed of.

The second year, I put on the full-court press and managed to get her to start dating me. Susan was exactly the girl I had been searching for all through my twenties: smart, beautiful, tough, different. After graduation, when finally I was able to head to California, Susan gave up what would have been a fantastic career in high-powered finance in New York City, loaded up her grandmother's old car, and followed me out there. We set up house in that studio apartment in Larkspur. She was the light of my life. I could not have been happier. I loved her dearly; still do. Eventually, in 1975, we bought a brand new little house nearby.

The house was small, and in a few years we started having babies, so we built a house across the freeway and raised our three fabulous kids in the little burg of Ross. In the end, though, there just wasn't sufficient compatibility between Susan and me, and I couldn't keep it together. I cycled through five counselors trying, and while the common thread that ran through all five was it's never a 100% one-sided problem, I nevertheless accept full responsibility for the loss, which I consider the biggest failure of my life.

CHAPTER THIRTY-FIVE

Leading Lady

When we started up Sonoma–Cutrer Vineyards, before the winery was built, our offices were in a rustic old bunkhouse in the vineyard. We had a hop kiln there and couple of other vintage buildings. The whole thing was so picturesque, movie companies or their location scouts would see it, and before you'd know it, they'd want to shoot movies in our vineyard. It got to be a real pain. I had a standard response for these guys: "First, you have to post a $1,500 bond." Otherwise, they'd trash everything. "Second, I want a walk-on part in the movie." The third condition was, "I get to sleep with the leading lady."

I told the office staff, "You don't even have to come to me. Just tell them those three conditions." It was a good way to get rid of them, and it worked fine until one day one of my people stuck her head around the corner and said, "We've got a movie company that wants to shoot in here."

"Told them the three conditions?"

"Yep."

"And?"

"They agree to two of them, but they don't want to post the bond." "Really? The other two conditions are okay?"

"Yep."

"What's the movie?"

"*The Magic of Lassie.* "

Oh well, I never wanted to be in the movies anyway.

CHAPTER THIRTY-SIX

The '80s

So, here we go. Sonoma–Cutrer Vineyards. SCV. Well, the investors wanted it, sure, but, in truth, the bug always bites vineyard growers. They sell their grapes to all these other guys and then watch the other guys go out and sell their grapes in the bottle and make a lot more money than the grape growers. At least, so it seemed. It looked so easy, making wine and making money. Stomp the grapes, make the wine, stick in bottles, go out and sell it. Make a lot of money and get famous. The bug bites all the vineyard growers and their families, and one by one they succumb. And then they find out it's not that easy.

So we succumbed also and said, "Okay, we'll have a winery," because we could see these 25 guys all doing well with our grapes. Of course, at that time, there was an explosion in white wine in the country. So it looked easy for us to just take the next step into the wine business with our own grapes. Estate-bottled Chardonnay.

In the late '70s, I tried to buy several wineries that were going bust. Souverain was one I almost got. Martini and Prati, another, was just a metal building with gravel floors. We got close to buying two or three others, but we just couldn't make a deal that made sense. At the time, Souverain was owned by Pillsbury, and they begged me to raise our bid just a little bit more. The night before they made a deal with North Coast Grape

Growers, they called me out of bed. I went down to San Francisco and met these guys in the lobby of their hotel. "Please, just raise your bid another half a million dollars." I wouldn't do it, so they did the deal with North Coast Grape Growers, and that didn't work out well. We decided we'd have to build our own winery from scratch. Hired the architect and off we went.

I didn't want to go around stealing people's winemakers, so I designed an advertisement for *Wines & Vines* that I thought would appeal to a particular winemaker, Bill Bonetti at Souverain. Bill was a classic Chardonnay winemaker. One day, the guy I dealt with to be the frontman in the ad called and said, "Hey, I got a resume here." It was Bill's, of course. Welcome aboard, Bill.

Sonoma–Cutrer Vineyards eventually became *the* Chardonnay winery in California. I decided to make the wine from only one variety. Well, we had a few cats and dogs in some small vineyard parcels, a little bit of Merlot and a little bit of Pinot, Riesling, others here and there. But I was impressed by Tom Jordan building a winery for Cabernet only, and I thought, *that's exactly the way it ought to be done.* So I designed ours for Chardonnay only. No sooner did we get going with that Tom Jordan added Chardonnay to his Cabernet mix. Anyway, we became the Chardonnay-only winery and got a fair amount of publicity because of that. Of course, the wine was damned good.

Jones family at Sonoma–Cutrer, 1987.
Left to right: Brice, Mom, Fithian, Marilyn, Dad, Emilia.

First Bottle of Sonoma–Cutrer, 1981.

CHAPTER THIRTY-SEVEN

Balls Out

I'm **Chuck Bennett.** I started working with Sonoma–Cutrer in 1983. They had not released anything yet. 1981 was the first vintage, and it was going to be released in the fall of '83. I came on board in the spring to set up marketing strategies. So we were working on the label and the roll-out plans. It was really exciting, partly because once you got in it and you realized what was going on, you knew how different Sonoma–Cutrer was and what a breakthrough it was going to be.

Brice got the idea for building croquet courts at Sonoma–Cutrer because he thought it would be an interesting publicity thing. You could have events there, and it would be something that would give him a unique angle for PR. Whenever he gets into something, he goes balls out. So he went down and met with a croquet club somewhere south of San Francisco.

He asked them, "If I build a croquet court at my winery as an event center attraction, would you guys come out and play there?"

Brice said the guy told him, "Not unless you become a croquet player yourself and join our club. We're not gonna do it just so you can take advantage of our croquet club."

So Brice became a croquet player himself. As they say, one thing leads to another, and he got just totally obsessed with building those courts, which are a very easily graspable visible metaphor for Brice's elaborate attention to detail in the winery and the winemaking process, some of which people could see if they took a tour, but many details you really couldn't see.

Now, as to the croquet courts, you could watch them being built, three or four layers of the right sort of substrates, everything exact and precise, dead perfect level. The world champion croquet player at the time said that they were the best croquet courts he had ever played on. So they're a good way for people to grasp just how committed Brice was to do things right, and, by extension, to make great Chardonnay.

Brice pretends he knows one end of
the mallet from the other.

To me, probably the most significant thing about Sonoma–Cutrer is its role in the history of post-World War II winemaking in California. It was the culmination of the American revolution in winemaking started by Robert Mondavi in the mid '60s. He left his brother, Peter Mondavi, of the Charles Krug Winery, and started his own winery because he wanted to do more traditional winemaking, using French oak and things like that.

By 1970, you had a group of the first generation of so-called "boutique" winemakers and owners who wanted to push that even further. You had people start looking at individual vineyards as part of the important makeup of the individuality of a wine. Chateau St. Jean was probably the first real commercial winery to start vineyard designating their Chardonnays. They had four or five from all different individual vineyards. Then toward the late '70s people started to think about narrowing their portfolios of wines. Up until that time, most people were still using the Baskin-Robbins approach to wineries. You had 31 flavors, you made everything.

Toward the end of the '70s, people began to realize that was not a traditional thing. In France, Burgundy makes only Pinot Noir and Chardonnay, Bordeaux makes only Cabernet or Claret wines, Germany only white Rieslings, et cetera. So this was another stage of maturation of the American wine business becoming more like the old world.

The first big commercial winery that really went to the extreme of producing one wine was Jordan Winery in Alexander Valley. Later, they watered it down by starting to make Chardonnay because they had a winery that was very traditional. It could've made anything. What they found was they had empty tanks and crushing facilities all sitting around earlier than the cabernet grapes would arrive, so it was just a huge temptation to go ahead and make Chardonnay as well. When Sonoma–Cutrer came along, they were the culmination of both those things. They had vineyard-designated wines, and they were only gonna make one variety, Chardonnay, in one winery that was built from the ground up for just one wine. Sonoma–Cutrer was designed from scratch to make Chardonnay. Everything about it, the cooling tunnels, the sorting tables, everything was designed for this specific variety. That was really new, and nobody could've driven that process better than Brice did, because he's an obsessive guy. When he got into this, he wanted to do everything the right way. And the "right way" meant what was right in the eyes of Bill Bonetti, who was S–C's first winemaker, just an incredibly fortuitous choice by Brice. Bill was such a great guy, so imaginative and inventive. And he had certain things he wanted.

Bill said that in Burgundy on the small estates, all the grapes were sorted by hand before they were pressed, so you'd get rid of any grapes not up to par. They would always pick at dawn so the grapes were really cool. Their cellars are always dirt floors so there's the right level of humidity in the cellar. On and on about these various things that really you should be doing. Don't crush the grapes first, you just press them with the whole clusters, and so on.

No one had ever attempted to make those kinds of processes scalable. They were all the way things were done in Burgundy, where the average family vineyard property is less than 10 acres. So these were all things that were traditional, but nobody had tried to figure out a way that you could barrel ferment 200,000 cases of Chardonnay or hand-sort several thousand tons of grapes.

Not only was the Sonoma–Cutrer winery specifically designed for one grape, it was specifically designed to reproduce all these laborious handcrafting techniques that had been traditional in Burgundy for centuries on a scale that no one had ever even thought about before. The result of that was that Sonoma–Cutrer opened doors for a whole lot of people. These days, it's not unusual to see wineries barrel ferment at large scale. Jones got people to start thinking, *"Wait a minute, there's not really necessarily a limit. If there's not a limitation on the grape supply, we shouldn't allow the engineering of the winemaking to be a stumbling block."* It was really an incredible achievement for Brice in that regard.

So the croquet courts were a metaphor for Brice's almost insane attention to detail that went into the development of the winery. There were a lot of times when it would've been easy to cut corners, and his investors wanted him to cut corners. They wanted to get this winery built, and the expenses kept getting higher and higher, and the cost overrun greater. Brice was always the buffer between the operations people at the winery and the investors. He never let Bill Bonetti down. If Bill wanted something, come hell or high water, Bill was gonna get it, no matter what it cost.

But Brice would try to find a way to make it more affordable. He'd negotiate with contractors, which he was very good at. The idea of not doing it was never an option. A lot of people give lip service to "no compromise." Almost everybody that gets into the wine business these days, especially people who have made a lot of money in another business and are doing this as a sort of capstone to their career or something for their own vanity will say they're setting their goals to make the best wine in the world, but as time drags on, and as expenses mount up, and as delays occur, and it takes so long to plan, so long making a wine, and then aging it and releasing it—all that stuff sort of goes by the boards. You can still make very good wine, but very few people have that attention to detail and a really serious commitment to it.

Brice was absolutely the right person for this project in every possible way. He just drove it to the absolute wall to get what he wanted. It was a real honor being a part of it. He wasn't the easiest guy to work for a lot of times, but he and I actually, I think, had fewer difficulties than most of the people there. I think Bill Bonetti and I probably got along with Brice the best and had the least difficulty.

Well, Bill you can understand because he got everything he wanted. Yeah, he did. He was also such a gentle guy. He looked like Einstein—a shock of white hair that stuck out at all angles. Bill was completely white-haired even when he was in his early 50s, maybe even late 40s. It gave him this classic little winemaker look. He looked the part so well, and he had a great Italian accent. He was the most gentle human being in the world, but he really knew what he wanted in terms of winemaking.

Brice's attention to detail and insistence on it really drove a lot of people nuts. He got into the fabrics for the curtains in the new office building, the placemats, the glasses, and every possible thing. Kind of hinges that would be on doors. Two-hour meetings about hinges. No, I don't want them to be glossy stainless steel, I want them to be satin finish. It just drove the contractors and people nuts.

But I happen to have a real OCD sort of mentality myself, so that never bothered me. I found it really good because it was highly useful when I wanted something or Bill Bonetti wanted something.

Mies van der Rohe, the famous German architect who was sort of the leader of the Bauhaus movement in the '30s, is famous for having said, "God is in the details." So, if that's true, then Brice would really be a holy man. But a much more common expression is that "the devil is in the details." If you look at it from that point of view, well then Brice is something else entirely.

Maybe he's both. Yeah, exactly. He is both.

The relevant characteristic for what Brice achieved in the wine business is just obsession with detail combined with an unbending obstinacy that he was gonna get what he wanted and that was just the way it was. And that's a good thing, especially if you're on the inside. I'm sure it came partly from his family background, career military officers and the kind of ideas of honor and duty and all that, but Brice had a really classical sense of, if you're inside my team, I am absolutely loyal to you, and I will go to the mat for you and not allow any outsider to attack or criticize you. If you're on the outside of that sphere, then everything is fair game.

He would've been a great general, a much better leader than manager. People worked for him and went to the mat for him and broke their backs for him because of that feeling of inspiration that great generals bring to the table, not because he was such a brilliant bureaucratic-style manager of people, you know? There was a totally different feeling, and it was great. It made us all feel, in those early days, like we were truly part of a team, not just paying lip service to it.

Bill Bonetti would come into my office every day, and we'd sit down and talk about stuff. He would ask me about winemaking and what he thought we should be doing. He was totally open, and vice versa. The vineyard manager and I would just talk all the time about everything. There were no interdepartmental jealousies or whatever. So it was really an honor to be part of it.

I never had any other experience even remotely like it in the wine business. I'd had several jobs before I came to Sonoma–Cutrer at age 31. Afterwards, I became a marketing consultant in the wine business, and I've had several dozen clients since then. I've been able to see how they work. Nothing even in the same ballpark in terms of the commitment to quality at all costs.

Brice loves that atmosphere in the workplace where everybody is involved with the entire mission. When the new winery was built, everybody had an office except for Brice. He didn't even want one. He had his office, so-called, I don't know what it was originally designed to be, a storeroom or something, on the first floor by the kitchen. Meanwhile, Ted Elliott, the controller, and I, the marketing guy, are upstairs in these really nice, well-appointed offices and Brice is down there. Likely as not, his door was open, and as likely as not, when I went down to see him, there'd be somebody sitting in there. He would either wave me in or say, "Give me five minutes."

Now, back to Brice. . . .

CHAPTER THIRTY-EIGHT

Five Guys and a Fax Machine

This tale is about the only overthrow of a marketing order in the United States, ever. It was the Wine Grape Marketing Order.

Marketing orders were created in the depths of the Depression as part of the New Deal. There were 55 or so of them in the country. None had ever been overthrown. Here's how they work: All the producers of various commodities get together in their own commodity-group, such as milk, avocados, butter, cranberries, and so on. The producers of each of these commodities say, "We're all going to put some money into the cranberry (or avocado, or milk, etc.) pot. And we'll have a board, and the board will find a way to promote avocados, or cranberries, or milk." Remember, these are commodities, not branded products. Although what some of these groups have done is brand their commodity, like Ocean Spray cranberries, Land O'Lakes butter, Chiquita Bananas, to try to make them a brand because advertising for commodities is highly ineffective.

One of the most successful marketing order commodities has been milk. But it's successful because thousands of dairy farmers put money into this milk-commodity pot, backed by the government. Once enough of the producers of each commodity band together and say, "We'll have a marketing order," then it's enforced by the government. Everybody who produces milk has to get into it and pays a tax. "Got Milk?" is a very successful promotion. All the dairy farmers see those trucks rolling along with pretty girls on the side of the truck, or they see the slogan on TV or on billboards, and they think that's what's selling their milk.

It isn't. What it's doing is taking a lot of that money in the marketing order pot and paying off congressmen to keep milk price supports up. I don't know how avocado and cranberry producers do it, but the big grape and wine producers thought they'd jump on the market-order bandwagon. They put in some money, and, because it's enforced by the government, all the small guys, who were doing just fine without the tax, had to ante up too. The tax is formulated by the big guys who make it most beneficial to themselves. The small guys pay disproportionately.

If the government weren't involved, the small guys wouldn't be putting in money, because they don't get enough benefit. They can brand their own avocados or grapes or whatever, or find their own one-on-one way to sell them at a roadside stand, farmers markets, and the like. So, the small guys don't ever really want to get in it. But the big guys need them in it, and need them to pay their "fair share." So that's why it's a marketing order, enforced by the government.

The guys on the commodity board like it because they are turning the big wheels in the advertising agency world, or promotions. And they get paid to be on the board. So as a rule, the big guys do it, and the small guys get dragged into it. It was the same with wine grapes. Gallo, Franzia, Wine Institute, these guys started it, and dragged all the small guys in.

Well, their timing was bad, because at that particular time in the late '80s, premium wine was beginning to collectively sell for more money than Gallo, Franzia, and all those big guys. Nevertheless, the big guys had all the hammers, and they rammed the Wine Grape Marketing Order through.

It was a California wine grapes marketing order, and they started TV advertising. I'll never forget this. The first commercial, maybe the only one, for all I know, had some what we used to call "yuppie" type guy sitting in a chair with a glass of wine in his hand, an upper-class dog curled at his feet. The yuppie looks straight down his nose at the camera and says, "Beer? My dog drinks beer. I drink California wine." This was possibly the stupidest advertisement in the world, but the big wheels on the board got to hang around and go to dinner with all these advertising suits and media dorks. Anyway, the marketing order got underway, and they were dinging all the producers of wine grapes. Naturally, the formula wasn't fair to the small guys but was loaded in favor of the big guys.

A couple of years after a new marketing order has been instituted, they have to have another vote with the whole industry participating. So five of us got together and said, "This thing has got to go." I remember it was Terrence Clancy, who was working for a big firm at that time; Bill McIver from Matanzas Creek; Patrick Campbell of Laurel Glen; Jess Jackson from Kendall-Jackson; and me. Fred Fisher from Fisher Vineyards occasionally joined us. Fortunately, Jess had all the resources and the money because we ended up having to sue the big guys, and government, too.

We started a campaign to vote the marketing order down. Bill McIver's wife, Sandra, had been a big wheel in the Democratic Party and knew how to mount a campaign, so she helped us. We bombarded every California wine producer with an endless stream of faxed flyers and calls to arms. That's how we got to be known as "Five Guys and a Fax Machine." It was the little guys against the big boys, and, by God, we did it. We overthrew the commission! The California Wine Grape marketing order went away—the only marketing order in the United States ever overturned.

Chapter Thirty-Nine
Focus on Chardonnay

In the fall of '83, we released the first Sonoma–Cutrer wines, all Chardonnay, of course. Our marketing arm was a national broker called Vineyard Brands. Robert Haas was the founder, owner, and president there, and he had about a dozen sales people around the country. He imported Burgundy, but he also wanted a couple of California brands. We had a meeting of the minds, and, gosh, he was such a gentleman. But I have to say, I think we pressed a little hard on getting the deal out of him we wanted, but he took it. He became the national broker for Sonoma–Cutrer, and he geared up and released the wine with us in the fall of '83.

Bob Haas was "Mr. Burgundy" in America. He used to appear on television with Orson Welles pitching Paul Masson Burgundy. Bob was a great guy. Maybe not a great negotiator, because we squeezed the hell out of him on our deal. But he did a great job. Never bitched about it, but he didn't extend the contract after it expired in five years. Being "Mr. Burgundy," he really knew all the wine guys in France.

Burgundy, up until that point, had been for me pretty much just a brand of Paul Masson. I didn't know anything about Burgundy. Not sure I had ever had a glass.

We used to have quarterly meetings with Bob to discuss Sonoma–Cutrer's progress and plans. At one meeting he said,

"Why don't we invite about a dozen Grand Cru Chardonnay producers from Burgundy in France to visit Sonoma–Cutrer?"

"Bob, do you think they'd come on their own nickel?" He said, "I'm sure they would."

Well, they did come, and on their own nickel. It was a pretty successful stunt, although we made it much more successful than when initially conceived. It got ten pages in *Wine Spectator* magazine, even though we downplayed it with the press. We didn't even release the news about it because, in order to get the French to come over, I told them this wouldn't be a PR stunt. It would be the real thing. We want to exchange information. We're going to have two dozen Chardonnay producers, half French and half American, and we're going to meet in seminar and do field trips and really explore for a week. To get them to buy into that, I thought it was necessary to say that there wasn't going to be any press here. "It's just an honest exchange of information."

Well, of course, the press did get wind of it and went ballistic when they couldn't get into our meetings. I'll never forget the San Francisco TV station guy, David Louie, banging down the door. When I jumped up and pushed the door shut, he stuck his foot in the way. He had a cameraman behind him taking shots over his shoulder, and he aired that clip on the evening news. A thrilling shot of a bunch of people drinking wine.

Robert Haas had wanted Sonoma–Cutrer in his portfolio because he thought we were very much in tune with the methods of Burgundy. *Focus on Chardonnay* was conceived as a PR gambit, but it became so much more. The French loved it, and Bob Mondavi did, too. Oh my God, he damn near killed people coming out of his driveway so fast one morning hurrying to get over to Sonoma County for the event. He came every morning, afraid he'd miss something. Anyway, our *Focus on Chardonnay* symposium was very successful, and it put Sonoma–Cutrer on the map. It was held in the summer of '86, the slow season, conceived as a one-time affair, but the participants all wanted to continue the tradition, so the group decided to do it every four years, alternating the venue between California and France, back and forth.

In 1990, we held it in Burgundy, and that was fascinating, especially for me. I couldn't believe how much the French knew about making wine and growing grapes. Of course, they had had 1,300 years of practice, but as Bob Mondavi said, "Well, if we'd started first, they'd have a hell of a time catching up."

We had the symposium back at Sonoma–Cutrer in '94 and did it again over there in '98. The next event would have been back at Sonoma–Cutrer in '02. I had sold Sonoma–Cutrer in '99. Got fired by Brown-Forman in '01, but they asked me back as a consultant to put it together for '02. I agreed to do it, for an arm and a leg, but the events of 9/11/2001 intervened, and the symposium got delayed a year. By then, Brown-Forman had had enough of paying me, so they did their version of it without me. They held it at Sonoma–Cutrer but included a lunch over at Angel Island. Some may say I crashed the party, but the French had invited me, so I went. *What's that saying about you can't get rid of a bad penny?*

Focus on Chardonnay. Bob Haas came up with the name and the concept, and it was a wonderful and productive experience, a couple of dozen Chardonnay producers, half of them

Burgundian and half of them American, guys like Bob Mondavi, Dick Arrowood, Bo Barrett, Steve Kistler. And the French were the usual suspects: Lafon, Fevre, Dauvissat, Leflaive, Morey, Matrot, Vincent, and Aubert de Villaine.

So there we were for the very first *Focus on Chardonnay* seminar in 1986 at Sonoma–Cutrer. There were no academics or government guys at the seminar, just producers. Each participant got up for an hour and talked about Chardonnay. We alternated speakers, French to American to French to American. The very first day, the very first speaker was a French guy from Chablis. About 35 years old, he had just inherited his domain. His name was Vincent Dauvissat. Vincent got up to give his talk, and he dug into his pocket and pulled out a handful of dirt. He held it out to the group and said, "This is my soil. Sun, rain, God...wine." And he went along about like that for his period. And then we tasted his wines with him.

The next guy was Dick Arrowood from Chateau St. Jean. He was Mr. Chardonnay in America at that point. He got up and popped a slide on the overhead and said, "This is my 33,000 BTU, stainless steel number four heat exchanger." That's the way this first seminar went. The French talked about their methodology and tradition and the Americans talked about technology.

But it was fascinating. When we went to Burgundy in 1990, as I say, I was blown away by their methodology and made a lot of friendships over there, which I've maintained through the years. One played a very important part in my life: Aubert de Villaine, the proprietor of the Domaine de la Romanée-Conti.

CHAPTER FORTY

Rootless

As I've said, the first *Focus on Chardonnay* seminar was at Sonoma–Cutrer in 1986, and the second was in 1990 in Burgundy. That's when my eyes were opened. I was really impressed by how much those guys knew about farming and making wine. As a result, I came home and changed everything we did from the UC Davis method to the Burgundian method: vineyard spacing, pruning method, trellising, crop load, fermentation time, and temperatures. We were already doing barrel fermentation, a huge change from the Davis method of stainless steel fermentation. We also began farming in the new French *biodynamique* method, a practice similar to, but not entirely the same as, organic, which has caught on big time in California since. Of course, in both biodynamic and organic, the use of chemicals is pretty much eliminated. But one of the main differences of biodynamic from organic farming is trying to get the vineyard floor to resemble that of a raw forest, earthworms and all. We don't do everything required in biodynamic farming— for example, we bottle when the wine is ready, not just under a new moon, and we stopped dancing naked under the full moon at midnight some time ago.

In 1994, the seminar was back at Sonoma–Cutrer. Now, when I was in Burgundy in 1990, I learned how much the French thought about the importance of their soil. I knew that they would be interested in our soils, so I went out behind the winery to a vineyard that had been planted in 1982, so it was 12 years old. The rows were eight feet apart, so the tractor could get between the vines to pull the harvested grapes and make for easy accessibility, and the vines in each row were about six feet apart. (We now plant 1 meter by 2 meters.) I went up there with a backhoe, and I had the widest bucket on the backhoe we had, which was 30 inches. I dug a trench between the vines, seven feet deep, 30 inches wide, and about nine feet long so you could walk gently down into the trench, down to seven feet, look at the soil on either side, and then walk up the other side to get out. There were about 30 inches between the wall of the trench and the vine.

I took all the French guys down into the trench (didn't bother with the Americans, who were not really into the terroir philosophy at that point). The French all dutifully walked into the trench and looked at the soil. Nobody said a word. I pulled aside one of the guys that I'd gotten a little close to, Dominique Lafon, whose wine is Comtes Lafon. I said, "Dominique, I don't get it. Nobody said a word." He said, "To tell you the truth, we're all a little surprised that we don't see any roots down there." He was right, there were no roots down there, but the significance just went right over my head, because I'd dug a lot of trenches in vineyards, a lot of holes, and I never saw a root. Well, when we started dry farming, I realized that when you irrigate with drip irrigation, as all California wine grape growers did, the roots all grow in a tight ball we call the "onion," an 18-inch diameter ball where water diffuses under the vine.

CHAPTER FORTY-ONE
A Piece of Land

It's 1994, the French just saw my "no roots" display. My blind spot regarding the significance of that still obscured my vision. Sonoma–Cutrer was just clicking along and kicking butt in the marketplace. A guy came into the winery and said, "I want to show you guys a piece of land out on the coast." I said I didn't want to drive all the way out there because it was a small piece, it was remote, and it would entail a whole lot of difficulties. Besides, the French have a saying, "You cannot make great wine if you can see the ocean from your vineyard." Years later, I asked a French retailer in NYC if he'd ever heard that saying. He shook his head. "No, but it makes perfect sense." I asked him to elaborate, and he explained that people like living near the ocean because they experience moderate daytime temperatures and warm(ish) nighttime temperatures. But grapes need warm days to mature (like 85°F.), and cool nights to retain the acids, which transpire out of the grapes over 50°F. at night.

The guy showing us the new piece of land, said the ocean was separated from the piece of land by the coastal mountain range, so it couldn't be seen from what would eventually be a vineyard. Despite my misgivings, I drove out there to the unincorporated town of Annapolis, population a couple hundred. The trip was a slow, winding hour, and when I got there I beheld 40 magical acres covered in legally clearable redwood trees. It had a nice slope, the right aspect-that is, the slope faced the right direction for maximum ripening quality. The site was just gorgeous. I envisioned a beautiful vineyard, but it was not going to be a Sonoma–Cutrer vineyard, because at that point we were working 1,100 acres of vineyards around Windsor, and I didn't want to set up a remote labor camp, remote tractors, remote management, and all that for 40 acres of vineyard out at the coast.

But it was going to be a beautiful vineyard for somebody, and I decided to buy it myself and put it in my son Victor's name.

Victor was having problems in high school, and he ended up dropping out at age 16. He passed the GED, and he figured he was smarter than the teachers, so why should he sit there in class?

To tell the truth, he's smart as a whip—probably the smartest kid in the family, smartest person in the family—but organized school and he did not mesh. I did send him for a year at WyoTech, a highly regarded school at the time for mechanics, and he pretty much aced that. He was interested, so he paid attention and applied himself.

At that point in 1994, I figured I'd put the land in his name. If things went south for Victor, he could always pitch a tent and live on it. So I bought it, put it in Victor's name, and just sat on it.

When I was selling Sonoma–Cutrer in July of '99, Sonoma County passed what they called a "hillside ordinance," which was a legal way of saying we don't want any more vineyards. Napa had had a hillside ordinance for 10 years at that point. Many folks out in western Sonoma County have the mindset the land belongs to the People, and they don't want to see anybody making a profit off the People's land.

So Sonoma County passed the Hillside Ordinance in '99, making it very tough to plant new vineyards. They did give us a year and a half to plant, if we had the plan in place. I was selling Sonoma–Cutrer, had a pocketful of money, could have done it myself, but I decided to take a partner. I approached one of my friends from Burgundy, Aubert de Villaine, proprietor of Domaine de la Romanée–Conti (DRC), and he said, "Sure, Brice, I'll be happy to do this with you, but just the two of us, fifty-fifty. No winery, just a vineyard." I called it A–B for Annapolis, where the vineyard was, and Bouzeron, Aubert's hometown in Burgundy. Eventually, A–B morphed into meaning Aubert & Brice.

For two years, while I was still president of Sonoma–Cutrer, before the new owners (Brown-Forman) fired me, I was trying to develop this vineyard out there absentee. It was painful, but it wasn't at the top of my priorities list, and Victor was getting the trees cut down and getting started. Victor loved the land, and he went out there to manage the development. He was eighteen years old and he was becoming a hermit. He liked being out there in the boonies, working for himself, and he worked hard on developing it—by himself. In due course I added (S–C's vineyard manager) Kirk Lokka's wife, Debbie, who graduated from Fresno State, a university with a very strong agricultural program, and the two of them worked it together.

Aubert and Brice seal the deal.

Chapter Forty-Two

The Whiskey Guys

In '91, Sonoma–Cutrer—the vineyards and winery—was 19 years old. Kent Klineman said it was time to sell. I balked. I was knee deep in my pursuit of Burgundian excellence. And I knew we were way premature in terms of the profitability we would see five or ten years hence. But Kent mounted a proxy fight, which I barely beat back, 51% to 49%. I then packed the board with Brice people: Sam Hardage, John Gray, my own father-in-law, but I could see the writing on the wall.

I began to realize that I was eventually going to have to sell the place or go public. In the mid '90s, I began putting out feelers about selling Sonoma–Cutrer. I didn't want to run a public company. I really felt I owed it to Kent to sell it. I could have pressed on and probably held on a while longer, maybe a few more years, maybe found a way to buy out enough guys to tide the vote over in my favor, but I really felt I owed it to Kent. He had been such a spectacular partner, doing everything he said he would do. He had assumed he'd get out in eight or nine years, although he was perfectly happy with the new winery. But then after that, he thought it was time to get out. I had three or four suitors including my friend, Jess Jackson of Kendall–Jackson. In the end I chose to sell to Brown-Forman, against the advice of my good friend, advisor, and Academy classmate

Sam Hardage, who said, "Sell it to the highest bidder." I didn't want to sell it to the highest bidder because they were going to get rid of me in six months and change the distributors, my loyal allies (I thought). For once, and the only time I can recall ever, I didn't take Sam's advice, because Brown-Forman sang this siren song: "We'll need you forever. You'll be running all of our wine division and blah-blah-blah, and we won't fire any of your distributors."

By the way, a good relationship with the distributors is rare. It's usually a confrontational relationship because their motive is to move boxes at any price they can get. Get 'em to the retailer, stack 'em high, and let them fly. My objective was *to build a Grand Cru brand,* and that's a totally different project. So Sonoma–Cutrer was unique. Our whole marketing program was the flip side of what everyone else was doing. We were going to build our brand in restaurants. Wine producers who had been dealing with distributors since the '50s said, "That's not how you build a brand. You go to retailers. They blow it out for you, and everyone becomes acquainted with it, and that's when they ask for it in restaurants."

My marketing guy, Chuck Bennett, knew better. He said, "We're going to do it backwards. We're going to go mostly to restaurants." The distributors begrudgingly went along, and in a few years they saw that it worked. They were making a lot of money, and retailers *begged* for Sonoma–Cutrer after it was successful in restaurants.

I had become personal friends with the presidents of the distributors, and I told Brown-Forman, "You can't fire my distributors because I have a relationship with these guys." And Brown-Forman said, "OK, we won't."

But they did.

They had a couple of wineries in California. One was Jekyl. Been out of business for a long time now. The other was Fetzer. Of the various suitors we had, I thought Brown-Forman knew the least about fine wine; therefore, they'd have to keep me for a long time. Well, I was half right. They knew nothing about fine wine, but they didn't keep me. Their modus operandi was to triple production, get grapes wherever they could, let the cases fly out the door, and wherever they landed was just fine. They didn't have the foggiest idea what that brand was all about, and the concept of grand cru was as familiar to them as the far side of the moon.

Of course, they did dump my distributors. In New York City, my friend, the president of the NY distributor, lost the brand while selling 22,000 cases of Sonoma–Cutrer per year in restaurants, which is unheard of. I mean, Gallo couldn't do that, Kendall-Jackson couldn't do that. Twenty-two thousand cases a year, and he got fired because Brown-Forman wanted to have the wine at the same distributor where the whiskey was. I tried to tell them that was dumb-dumb-dumb, but they were in the whiskey business. They didn't give a rat's (bleep) about the fine wine business. It was just a dividend check to them. Anyway, having decided to sell the company to these whiskey guys, how long do you think I lasted? I had a five-year contract. The office pool said 18 months.

Well, they canned me after two years and brought in their own people, who didn't know fine wine from Slurpee.

I went back to a business school reunion a few years ago, and one of my classmates, Steve Schwarzman, who had founded Blackstone, just about a trillionaire, was there. I said to him,

"Steve, you know I kind of wish I'd gone public instead of selling, because at least I'd still be there."

Steve shook his head. "No, you wouldn't still be there. You probably lasted longer selling it than you would have with a public company." After Mondavi went public, within about a year, they started sending in the Harvard Business School guys, and they ran it into the ground.

I didn't realize how powerful the Sonoma–Cutrer brand was when I sold it. If I'd been able to hold onto it all this time, it'd be a half billion dollar brand now. But I couldn't, and I sold it because I thought it would be the right thing to do for Kent. There might have been other ways we could have accomplished that, but selling it was the most straightforward. So I sold to the Jack Daniel's guys!

I'm restraining my impulse to say more on this subject.

CHAPTER FORTY-THREE

The "Bad Guy" Exits

I'**m Michael Lavenson.** I started with Brice in 1988. In July of 2001, he was asked to leave the property. During that time I was national sales manager.

There were two rock stars in California wine. Brice was Mick Jagger. Robert Mondavi was more like John Lennon. Brice was more "The Bad Guy." I remember him selling Sonoma–Cutrer to Brown-Forman at landmark prices then telling them to go (bleep) off. That was in 1999, and he was hired to stay on as president of the winery. He was being asked to deliver financial reports on a regular basis, as did all of Brown-Forman's companies, Jack Daniel's being probably the biggest. Brice would just disregard these requests. He felt having a large accounting office was too stressful. Of course, he had already sold the company. At that point, the feeling was that people admired Brice because he stood up to the big company in a way they had never heard of before.

By law, we sell to distributors, and the restaurants are the end buyers, and Brice figured out a way to create loyalty with the end consumer in a way I've never seen anyone else do without marketing on TV.

I totally appreciate Brice's attention to detail. If I asked him, "What do you mean" about certain things or situations, he would say, "Well, just think what an uncompromising winemaker like the Baron Philippe de Rothschild would do with that question you're asking me, and when you figure out what he would do, that's what the answer is."

I was very comfortable with that, because it set a standard and a pace that, well, you know, it's integrity. There's no attention to detail that is missed. There's no cutting of the process that hasn't been exhaustively thought out.

Now over to Jim Hinkle . . . .

CHAPTER FORTY-FOUR

Croquet and Ejection Seats

I'm **Jim Hinkle.** I didn't know Brice at USAFA. At our 15th reunion in 1976, I renewed my friendship with Bob Brickey, who had been my roomie for a semester. He was good friends with Brice, and I got invited to join them at Randy Kennedy's home in NJ to attend the Air Force-Army game. I was then invited to join a group of reprobates called the Winos and Derelicts (WDs), who gathered every spring for skiing. Copious amounts of Sonoma–Cutrer were consumed every year. Starting in the early 2000s, we skied at Telluride and stayed in the BCJ mansion. 2017 was the last year that the Winos and Derelicts met at Brice's. For some reason, he sold his house right out from under us.

My daughter Christina was born with Down Syndrome in February, 1985. The following winter, in the middle of a Denver snowstorm, Brice appeared at our door with a beautiful, gift-wrapped little dress. Then he said that he and Sonoma–Cutrer were going to do a World Croquet Championship tournament, and the proceeds were to go to Down Syndrome charities. The first year, 36 players came from all over the world. My family was invited and treated like royalty. The tournament was grand, but the spectator turnout was sparse. Robert Mondavi and other wine people were there.

The tournament evolved over the next 15-plus years into an extravaganza, a real party and fundraising event with 1,500 spectators all dressed in white. A number of restaurants catered very tasty morsels. Many wine producers donated their wines and dinners at their wineries for auction. There were silent auctions and there were live auctions.

When Brice was terminated by Brown-Forman in 2002, there was a "retirement event" at the winery. A group of the 61st Tactical Fighter Squadron (Mythical) secretly attended. Sam Hardage, myself, Lanny Lancaster ('62), Bill Kosco (USMA), Rich Mayo, Frank Kiszely, and Gene Stringer were hidden down the hill from the retirement celebration. All of the S–C employees wore maroon baseball caps to signify the Pinot Noir that he was going to be making at his new winery. They all lined up to thank Brice, shake his hand, and wish him well. There was a "missing man" fly-by consisting of two Cessnas followed by a B-25 and then a 21-shotgun salute. They played taps and lowered the flag. That was our signal to run up the hill and take Brice prisoner. When we tackled him, he looked up at us in total disbelief. We sat him in an ejection seat on a flatbed truck, stuck a pilot's helmet on his head, and the group of us rode with him as he was paraded in front of all of his employees. Then we proceeded to neighbor Saralee Kunde's where we boarded cars and drove to Brice's new vineyard. It had been an apple orchard for, I think, 64 years. Sitting on the property was a metal building, on Gravenstein Highway. In it was a huge container of apples. We ate some and they were very good, foreshadowing the grapes that would come from the new vineyard.

Now back to Brice . . . .

CHAPTER FORTY-FIVE

Rising from the Ashes

The very same week I was signing Sonoma–Cutrer over to Brown-Forman in July 1999, Don Hallberg walked into the S–C winery and said, "I'm ready to sell, and you said you'd match any offer." Kirk and Debbie had been working on Don Hallberg for five years. The Hallberg Ranch was the most beautiful, fabulous 100 acres of potential great Pinot Noir land left, not only in Sonoma County, but in the North Coast and for that matter, California and the United States. And it wasn't cheap. We ended up paying double what I had expected. I had told Don I'd match any offer. Well, that turned out to be just about double the market price. He grew apples and sold pies out the front door. The orchard was on both sides of Hwy 116, the main north/south artery in western Sonoma County. But the Hallbergs were well into their 80s and ready to move on to other things. The going rate for orchard land was $28,000 an acre. The price should have been $28,000 an acre for an apple orchard. We ended up paying $44,000. I offered it to Brown-Forman, but they said no thanks, they didn't want to buy any more fixed assets. I said, "Do you mind if I do it?" They said go ahead, and I said just sign my "non-compete agreement right here," and they did.

Well, I had to agree to several "requests" by Don and Marsha Hallberg: "Would you leave our foreman in his house for life?" Don asked Kirk. "Yeah, we would."

"Would you leave my Liquidambar trees up my driveway?"
"Yes. Even though they are in the vineyard, yes."

We lost the Hallbergs about three or four years after the sale closed. The Liquidambars still grace the driveway and shed and grow into the vineyard adjacent. The foreman died a few years after Don and Marsha. The foreman's son lives in the house now. We're not going to kick him out. Just not gonna test any of that karma.

So we bought the Hallberg Orchard for the unheard of price of $44K an acre. Made the front page of the business section of the *Press Democrat* newspaper. People called me up: "Jones, you're raising the price for everybody who's looking to buy! Not only that, but you're messing up the tax base for everyone else. You stupid (bleep)! What the hell is wrong with you?"

Well, thanks to my sale of Sonoma–Cutrer, I had the money. I bought the Hallberg land and then went out to raise money to put together Goldridgepinot, which was to be the next chapter in the life of Brice Cutrer Jones. But first, for one brief and not so shining moment, I was the president of Brown-Forman's recent acquisition, Sonoma–Cutrer. In July of 2001, when the whiskey guys gave me my walking papers, I trundled five miles west to Hallberg's Orchard. B-F kindly fired a few guys who were deemed too loyal to me, and they boogied west as well. Within six months, most of the rest quit and moved over to my new venture. Inasmuch as the entire team at that point, sans winemaker, was from Sonoma–Cutrer, we changed our name from Goldridgepinot to Emeritus Vineyards. Kirk Lokka had been with me since 1982. He was our VP/Vineyard Manager and is now not only that but also our General Manager.

Michelle Sweet started at S–C in 1995, a master of event planning and perfectionist extraordinaire. She knows everything there is to know about the wine business in general and Emeritus in particular. She practically runs the place.

Ted Elliott started at S–C in 1982 as CFO, moved up to Executive VP and my right-hand man. Still does an incomparable job. What a guy! And the viticulturist/horticulturist at S–C, Don Moore, said wherever I went, he wanted to come along, so I put him to work at Emeritus. But I had further plans for him at the coast.

CHAPTER FORTY-SIX

What Do You Mean, Irrigation?

After moving my desk over to Emeritus, I flew to France and got together with Aubert in Beaune and said, "I want to buy you out, Aubert. It's not fair to you. We've got way too much money tied up in this. I've only got seven of the forty acres planted, straggling up the stake, and I don't even have an irrigation system in yet." I pulled the check out for his half of the deal, and he was reluctant to take it, even though it was a pretty sizeable amount of money for only seven acres of vineyard, and we didn't even own the land. Victor still owned it, and we leased it from him. Aubert reluctantly took the check and said, "Oh, you know, this is not so bad. The cheapest land in Burgundy is Pommard, and it's $800,000 an acre." While we weren't in that ballpark, I mention this because of what Aubert said to me next.

"Irrigation system? What do you mean irrigation?"

"Don't give me that, Aubert. You have summer rainfall here in Burgundy. Every wine-growing region in the world has summer rainfall—*except California*. If we don't irrigate, we'll kill the vineyard." In fact, we had tried it at S–C a few years earlier, at Les Pierres. We pulled the water off, or at least reduced it, but we did almost kill the vineyard.

He said, "Maybe so, but if you irrigate you will change the signature of the wine."

Huh? The signature of the wine?

So Aubert planted in my head the seed of future revelation, which I let germinate for a good two years, trying to figure out what he meant by changing the signature of the wine. Eventually, I decided I knew what Aubert meant and I went to Kirk. "I think I know what Aubert meant by that 'change the signature' business," I said. (I actually didn't then, but do now). "I think we oughta dry farm." Kirk said, as any California farmer likely would have. "You know we can't dry farm. We don't have summer rainfall, and we'd kill the vineyard."

"Well, Kirk, I've been thinking about this a while, and this ranch we farm now, Hallberg Ranch, was in vines before prohibition, and they didn't have an irrigation system."

He said, "Yes, but the housewife had to come out on weekends with a teapot."

"Okay, what are you and Debbie doing this weekend?"

Kirk agreed (not to Debbie and a teapot), but he said we'd take five years to pull the water off, not one year.

We lost 40% of our production for three years running as the vines were weaned off the water, but Kirk got us there, and our first fully dry-farmed vintage was 2011, a super vintage for us, unlike the rest of the growers, whose (irrigated) grapes produced what the press called the "Vintage from Hell." That was because it was a very cold summer, nobody's grapes ripened on time, rain was forecast for October 5th, and the unripe grapes had to go through that rain. They didn't really weather it well—in fact, they developed a lot of rot. But guess whose grapes were off the vines a week before the rain! I came back from buying out Aubert in Beaune and rolled the A–B Vineyard into the new Emeritus enterprise. I called it the William Wesley vineyard after my father, William Wesley Jones. I put Don Moore out there as vineyard manager, reporting to Kirk, but he was perfectly comfortable living the life of a hermit. And it did become a beautiful vineyard and produced some of the county's finest Pinot Noir. Emeritus got top dollar for the grapes, and used about 25% of the production for the Emeritus William Wesley Pinot Noir. After a good and sustained run with WW as our top wine, we sold the vineyard in 2014 because we were on the verge of losing money on it. While the grapes were unequaled in quality, the vineyard was too remote. It had always been too remote, and labor and distance were too expensive. Grape buyers hated driving out there to inspect their grapes, and eventually they drifted away. It became a money-losing piece, but, on the upside, it did produce fabulous grapes, and Victor had spent what I know were pleasant times there, and I did name it for my father.

In 2014, the vineyard was just what was needed for Judy Jordan, owner of "J," to amp up her Pinot brand. But about six months after she bought it from us, she sold her entire operation, vineyards and all, to Gallo. So it's not likely we'll ever see another William Wesley Pinot from that land. 2015 was our last vintage.

CHAPTER FORTY-SEVEN

Cracking the Egg

I'm Sam Hardage. Brice is an Academy classmate, friend, and business associate. Here's how that last part happened:

I was living in LA at the time, and Brice came down and said he was going to get into the farming business and grow grapes to make wine. I was curious about how serious he was about the whole thing. Well, he was pretty darned serious, and he set about it in a singularly focused way. And by gosh, he got it done. After that conversation, I said count me in. That was about as serious as we got about financial objectives. This was just before he started buying land and ended up with about 1,150 acres.

That turned out to be quite a propitious decision at the time, because grape land in Napa and Sonoma was pretty reasonable back then. In fact, it was very reasonable, considering what it is right now. You couldn't do today what we did then. It would be impossible. I shouldn't say that. It wouldn't be impossible if you were the Koch brothers or the Microsoft boys. You could do it, but it would be insane, because it would cost *waaay* too much! The decision to buy land to grow grapes to make Chardonnay, at that particular moment, turned out to be a very good decision indeed. I don't know if Brice was prescient or just lucky, but he knew what he wanted to do: buy land to grow grapes. And then he wanted to learn how to make wine.

And here's the important part He wanted to do it better than anyone else.

Through all the processes, the starts and stops and pluses and minuses, and everything else that we went through at Sonoma–Cutrer, and even today at Emeritus, Brice has always been on an unending quest to make better wine, and make the process better. The most unusual part of all this is that he really wanted to share this newfound knowledge with others.

I remember when he decided he wanted to do this "colloquium" on wine. An audacious effort because the French have always believed that in the wine world they are the beginning and the end, the alpha and the omega. Now, along comes this newbie who wanted to have this symposium on wine and invite the Frenchies over here so we could learn from them and they could learn from us. I was surprised the Frenchies wanted to hear what the Americans had to say, because there wasn't anything they didn't already know. The process opened up their eyes and ears and made them realize that, *Holy (bleep)*, we may have the name and the panache and all that kind of stuff, but these people are tossing out the old rules and in the process making things better, and they might catch up to us!" Brice really woke 'em up.

The competitive process stayed friendly, and the French became more interested in what was going on in wine country, good wine country like Sonoma and Napa, and that interest has continued to this day. You gotta give credit to Brice for opening that communication between the French and the California wine producers.

When Brice introduced his first wine to them, I held my breath. Well, they loved it! Brice really cracked the egg wide open on that one! There are a lot of close relationships today that the French have with producers, growers, vintners, and winemakers in Napa and Sonoma. The French ended up learning a lot from the Americans!

Brice says it took him 35 years to break the code on how to make world class vino, but unless you have the curiosity and the drive, you can spend all those years gaining "experience," but nothing will have changed. So the fact is that from the get-go, he really wanted to make it better, and he kept experimenting and never stopped experimenting.

Now back to Brice . . . .

Chapter Forty-Eight

Terroir

Terroir is a French term by which all great wines are described world-wide. Terroir is the sense of place unique to each great wine. The rap on California wines is that they don't express terroir. I, along with all the other wine growers in California, always used to say B.S. to that.

Here's the French concept of terroir: Three elements make up terroir: Soil, Climate, and Man. Soil gives the wine its character. Climate gives the wine its personality. Man gives the wine its spirit. Like a three-legged stool, the three elements have to be about equal, or the stool falls over. At the same time, Man is the most important of the three because he can manipulate the *effects* of the other two elements.

I think about these three elements this way: If you're from a family of 10 kids, those 10 kids all have similar character because they have similar roots. They have different personalities because of what influences them outside the home. They're introverted, extroverted, athletic, whatever, but it has nothing to do with their heritage, their common roots, or their parents. Soil gives character. Climate gives personality. Man gives the wine its spirit. For 20 years I translated "spirit" to "style." It was only about 8 or 10 years ago I developed a deeper understanding. I was riding the Telluride chairlift with a bartender who was a Master Somm, and I said, "Hey, Nick, what do you think about the idea that Man gives wine its spirit?"

"Oh, that's very obvious," he said, puffing on a steel pipe. "Man gives it the spirit." That got me nowhere but lost, so later I went down to his bar in one of Telluride's best restaurants, and picked his brain for an hour. I came away with a little more understanding about the concept that "Man gives wine its spirit."

It's 1994, the third *Focus on Chardonnay* seminar. We're back at Sonoma–Cutrer, all 24 of us sitting around a conference table, where we're going to "blind" taste everybody's wine. Robert Haas, Mr. Burgundy in America, and Jacques Puisais, the French National Director of Taste, who taught me all this about terroir, are the co-moderators. They'll start with the wines, everybody will taste, and then we'll all talk about them.

Robert Haas starts. He picks up a glass, and I happen to know that it's our wine, Les Pierres, Sonoma–Cutrer's top of the line. Haas picks it up, sips it, puts the glass down and says, "Wow! It's great to taste a California wine with terroir."

A well-known Napa producer goes ballistic, "My wine has terroir. My wine has terroir. It's got north Napa and south Napa terroir combined." I knew Robert Haas was right about our wine, but I also kind of agreed with the Napa producer about his. What did I know? We were still irrigated at that point.

But you know what? Bob Haas *was* right, and the reason American wines *couldn't* show terroir is that all of the grapes came from vines grown from irrigated vineyards. Consider that the water from the drip irrigation emitters diffuses under each vine in about an 18-inch sphere, which we call "the onion." It couldn't form in the Les Pierres vineyard because there's very little soil there, the land being an old rock quarry. The onion is where all the roots grow. Why would they go elsewhere? The roots grow in the onion. Problem: horticulturally speaking, the mass of the roots of any plant must be about equal to the mass of the vegetation above ground for the roots to sustain the plant. When all the roots are growing in the onion, their mass is NOT equal to the mass of all the vegetation. Consequently, the farmer must re-wet the onion every few weeks. During an average summer, he may apply three, even four, irrigations. Eventually, after we became dry farmed, I realized that with irrigation, we had been growing the vines essentially hydroponically. Finally, I understood Aubert de Villaine's admonishment, "If you irrigate, you will change the signature of the wine."

The difference in the signature of the wine Aubert referred to with irrigation, as opposed to no irrigation, turns out to be significant.

The onion.

Compare the flavor of a hothouse tomato to a Sonoma County garden-grown tomato, and you'll see what I'm talking about.

Dry-farmed cutaway shows roots spreading.

A couple of years ago, *Forbes* magazine published an article on dry-farmed vineyards. Out of some 4,000 California vineyards, they identified six or eight of them as dry farmed, of which of course, Emeritus was included.

In any case, the rap on California wines is they don't have terroir. Well, they've got the Climate all right. They may have the Man part. But, they don't have the Soil, the character, because the vines are being irrigated.

I was in New York a few years ago selling Emeritus wine. I was already well into dry farming. In all the restaurants I went to, all these heavy duty sommeliers were saying, "Your wine is great. It's very Burgundian. But, I'm not picking up all that red fruit that I'm accustomed to in the other Russian River Valley Pinots."

I chewed on that a bit and concluded, "You know, all that red fruit is there in our wine, but it's integrated so well with the character of the soil that the red fruit is not the *predominant* characteristic of the wine, as it is with almost everybody else's." So, the predominant characteristic in those other California wines is the red fruit personality from the Climate. It's there in our wine; it's just not the predominant characteristic.

The long and the short of it is that at Emeritus we have all the elements of terroir—Soil, Climate, and Man—like a three-legged stool, in about equal importance: in balance.

CHAPTER FORTY-NINE

My All Wet Grand Cru Dream

Back to 1994, the third *Focus on Chardonnay*: We're holding it at Sonoma–Cutrer for the second time. Before I take the French down in my trench so they can see nothing but dirt (no roots), I give them my hour-long presentation: *California: Soil, Climate and Man* (the three components of terroir).

I lead off with *Soil*. I've got maps and charts of how the western part of North America was formed. I want to take a bunch of Burgundian wine producers, who have just had breakfast and are in a time zone eight hours earlier than what they're used to, on a 500-million-year journey through Island arc drift, subduction of the Farallon Plate beneath the North American Plate, magma, the volcanic Ring of Fire, the formation of California and the great wine growing region of Napa, Sonoma, and Mendocino counties, all underlaid by the Franciscan Melange, which contains rock from the entire Pacific Basin, accounting for a wide variation in soils from one vineyard to the other.

After *Soil*, I'm on *Climate*. I explain the formation of mountain ranges, resultant air flow, precipitation, soil drainage, temperature variations, the Coast Range, the Central Valley, and the Golden Gate.

Then I discuss *Man*. I whisk through 7,000 years, from the Bering Strait migration to the early Spanish settlers, to 1812, when the Russians established a settlement at Fort Ross on the

Sonoma Coast and actually grew grapes until they left in 1840. They were here to trap otters, and after they killed them all off, the Russians left, leaving their vineyards behind. Latter-day vineyards in Sonoma County, though, proliferated mostly in areas warmer than the Coastal area, outside the marine influence.

Yes, I know I'm barreling through millenia, skipping ahead so I can get to the wrap-up of my *Focus on Chardonnay* presentation, verbatim from the transcription:

MR. JONES: The Sonoma Coast topography ranges from flat to steep, as in the Côte d'Or. There are exposures, that is, the aspects of the slopes, to all points of the compass. True, we don't have limestone here, but we have rocks from the Sonoma volcanics. The hillsides in Sonoma Coast with the proper slope, exposure, soil structure, water management, and other man-controlled aspects (such as pruning, density of planting, and yield control) may just produce wines that my grandchildren might consider in the genre of grand crus. I don't say we make grand crus, but that is what we are aiming for, and we are learning as best we can. At least my grandchildren might understand a little better than we do today. I wish we had the experience of 700 years. We don't, and we only get one crop a year. But we're trying pretty hard.

With that, I can take questions or talk about any aspect of this. A lot of this will be talked about as the week unfolds, but if there is anything at all now, please bring it up and we'll talk about it briefly. Also, it is a distinct honor to have Bob Mondavi here to ask any questions about Napa Valley.

MR. HAAS: *I think there's one point that you probably meant to say, but you missed, and that is that the 30 inches—which is what, 600 or 650 millimeters—of rain a year [in the Sonoma Coast] all happens in about four months. It happens like November, December, January, February, and maybe a little in March; after that, nothing.*

MR. JONES: *Yes. In California if you are growing grapes on a hillside, if you don't irrigate, the vines will die. That's a pretty general statement, and maybe there are some exceptions somewhere to that. I don't know about them. But we have tried it, and we were killing the vines. So I think on hillsides, you have got to irrigate in California.*

Hah! Remember, this was in 1994. I didn't know that 17 years later, I would have my first vintage of fully dry-farmed California Pinot Noir.

Moral of the story? The more you think you know, the more egg you might end up with on your face.

CHAPTER FIFTY

Orina de Caballo

I'm **Gerry Dawes.** One of the first things I heard come out of Brice Jones's mouth was a lawyer joke. After I spent a whole day with him, running around the streets of New York selling Sonoma–Cutrer, and hardly hearing Brice utter a word, we went to dinner at Jams and sat at a table in the upstairs dining room. He had invited one of his major investors, a lawyer named Kent Klineman, to the dinner. Jones had remained quiet and, I thought, sullen. Then Klineman arrived, and the first words out of Brice's mouth were: "Klineman, do you know the difference between a dead skunk and a dead lawyer in the road?"

"No."

"There are skid marks in front of the skunk!"

Jones cracked up. Klineman shrugged it off, as if he was used to abuse from Brice.

So I said to myself, well, maybe he's not so bad after all. (Over the years, I have come to question my own judgment on that score.) You see, he'd come to New York with a reputation, plus he'd gone to Harvard Business School, and he'd approached our veteran sales staff at Winebow in New York and New Jersey with his sales plan and we were all bitching to the high heavens about what a demanding (bleep) he was. We were unhappy because it was a computerized system where we had to account for how much every single account was using, what we thought the average was going to be on a yearly basis. Just a whole lot of extra work. It was a system that none of us had ever seen.

Well, it turned out to be genius, because apparently Brice knew what the hell he was doing, and this is what built Sonoma–Cutrer into America's most sought-after Chardonnay.

Anyway, Jones and I became fast friends because of that, and we still are. Early on, he invited me, an ex-United States Navy enlisted aircrewman Russian linguist ("enlisted puke," he called me) to join him and his "occifer" (I called them) buddies and their wives, girlfriends and the occasional farm animal to attend the biennial Army-Air Force games at West Point and to their Bacchanal party weekends in November around the game. I have been an active participant for some 30 (I shudder) years now. Like I said, I'm a United States Navy (God Bless!) man, so I refer to Brice and his group of Air Force Academy and Air Force guys as "Zoomies" and sometimes a few other epithets that are unprintable. And twice I've taken a group of the Zoomies to Spain, a country I have been living or traveling in for more than 50 years, leading them on gastronomy, wine, and cultural adventures around my adopted country.

Jones and I have had many, many adventures, including a time when his wife was gone and he was watching his kids, who were holy terrors in his hands (one of them graduated from West Point), and he's got no matches or anything to light the barbecue, and we're running back and forth from the kitchen stove through the house and out to the patio with rolled up newspapers that we were lighting from the kitchen burners. Well, one of Brice's little boys decides to imitate us and help out by lighting a newspaper, which began to unfurl and flame up, so he dropped it in the middle of Brice's wife, Susan's, white kitchen floor, which caused Brice's sister Emilia, who was wearing sandals, to try to try to stomp it out, burning her foot and generally failing to put it out before it had made a big scorched spot in the middle of the floor. I grabbed a pan of water and poured it on the burning newspaper, but it was too late. Brice then came in, saw the scorched floor, and knew that when Susan came home there was going to be Hell to pay, at which point, he began to give his sister Emilia hell, which caused me, in her defense, to tell him if he did not leave Emilia alone, I was going to take him outside and wallop his ass in the mud!

So apparently when Susan came home after that weekend, she was apoplectic at seeing the scorch mark the burning newspaper had made on her pristine white kitchen floor. Apparently, being a Harvard Business School graduate, Brice took the most intelligent remedy he could think of to the situation: blame it on the goddamn swabbie, the Navy enlisted man, Dawes. Susan rarely spoke to me after that, and when she did, it was with a certain disdain.

One night, on Army-Air Force weekend, we had dinner at the Thayer Hotel at West Point after the football game. Brice's old friend Lanny Lancaster and I got up and began to analyze Brice's Chardonnay, Sonoma–Cutrer Russian River Ranches. I held a glass of the wine up to the light and very seriously said, "Look, folks, I want to give you all some lessons on how to evaluate Brice's wine. This is how you taste and judge a wine."

I was a wine and food writer who wrote for a number of wine and food magazines, so I had some credibility. I said, "First, you hold your glass up to the light to see the color. Now you see this classic color that we call in Spanish, *orina de caballo*, or horse (bleep)." And then it went downhill from there. And then you get the horse (bleep) coming through in the nose, and then it comes through in the palate, and then we just started tearing Brice's wine apart, comparing it not just to horse (bleep), but to gasoline, etc.

But anyway, all those things aside, Jones has an incredibly bio-worthy life, if nothing else, as a roadmap for other people about how not to live. The success story with Sonoma–Cutrer is remarkable. Brice held to his beliefs about this stuff, and he was right. As usual, he got the last laugh. He sold Sonoma–Cutrer for $140 million [author's note: only a fraction came to me, and the government raked off about half of that], then he bought not a Porsche, a Maserati or an Aston-Martin, but a goddamned Corvette (he still thinks he is back in the 1960s), an airplane (after promising his wife that he was done with flying), and he built a way too big, expensive albatross of a house in Telluride, Colorado.

So anyway, he sells Sonoma–Cutrer for banzai buckaroos, finally pays his long-suffering investors some money, and then, after buying the Corvette, the airplane and the Telluride ski house, he decides to (bleep) away the rest of the money by starting to make Emeritus Pinot Noir, a red wine, after he had made his name as a white wine guru.

When he had Sonoma–Cutrer, Brice declared that red wine was forbidden at our Zoomie gatherings, and I would, of course, always bring red wine. Now he's trying to forbid white wine, so I always bring several bottles of white wine, so the Zoomie wives and girlfriends crowd around my table to get some drinkable vino.

But in any case, Brice starts making this red wine, and then white wines are off limits. He's got a purely Republican, Trump soul. Whatever's good for me in this moment. I've actually got a few friends who are Repugnicants, famous people too, but I sort of sidestep politics when I'm around them. I mean, if it's Jones, I'd say anything, because insulting Jones is a national sport, as it should be, because he is so deserving.

Despite his politics, which is hard for me to figure out, Brice is incredibly generous and caring to his friends and others. They all just swear by him, so it's like there's two sides to the coin.

He's incredibly generous and an incredibly good friend. When my daughter was having a problem, he said, "Do you think it would help if I gave her my Corvette?" It was a crazy offer, but it just shows you how Brice can be. He was willing to give her his precious Corvette, even though there was no rhyme or reason to it. Just because he cared and wanted to help.

I told him no, because it would not have done her any good at the time (and I was hoping for an Aston-Martin, which I would have accepted and taken an equity loan out to buy my daughter a Toyota Corolla), but that is Brice for you.

And now, back to Brice. . . .

Gerry Dawes (top left with glasses) and the Zoomies.
The 61st Tactical Fighter Squadron (Mythical) celebrates
with wine bottle caps in their eyes.

CHAPTER FIFTY-ONE

Don Blackburn

So now that you know about terroir and dry farming, I'm going to tell you about Don Blackburn, the "man" element of terroir for our wine. In 1998, the fourth *Focus on Chardonnay* was scheduled to take place in Burgundy. This would be our second symposium over there. By then, Bob Mondavi was long in the tooth, and Mike Grgich (owner of a well-regarded Napa Chardonnay) had gone back to Croatia, so I needed a couple of replacements. Chuck Bennett told me about this guy down in Monterey County at a winery called Bernardus. His name was Don Blackburn, and I knew, judging from the quality of Chardonnay he was putting out, he was a pretty good winemaker. At that time, I didn't know anything else about him. I didn't know that he had gotten his enology degree in Burgundy at Dijon and had worked for the next 10 years up and down the Côte-d'Or, making wine. I just knew he was making good Chardonnay.

Called him up. "Hi Don, Brice Jones here. You wanna join us for this seminar in Burgundy, *Focus on Chardonnay*? Everyone gives a one-hour presentation, something to do with Chardonnay, and you have a tasting of your wine to illustrate your presentation."

He was intrigued and agreed to participate. The night before his presentation in Burgundy we met and had dinner. I asked him if he was ready, and he assured me he was. He didn't say what he had in mind, just that he was raring to go.

The next day, 24 Chardonnay producers, French and American, gathered for the symposium. When it was Don's turn to make his presentation, he was nowhere to be seen. It occurred to me that maybe I should have vetted this guy more thoroughly. There was a booth in the back of the room where a couple of hired guns translated contemporaneously from French to English, English to French, depending on the speaker. After an endless two minutes of ominous silence, Don's voice came through the earphones (from inside the booth). He said everything in both English and French, translating back and forth on his own.

"Ladies and gentlemen, you have eight glasses of white wine in front of you, and a piece of paper. Turn over the paper." We did. There was a common enough tasting grid, A, B, C, D, E, across the top for the wines, and down the left side, to be matched to each wine, one at a time, were listed (not common at all) ten pieces of classical music. He proceeded to play each piece through the earphones. The exercise was to match each of the wines to the musical composition that these world-class wine producers felt was the best match.

The French were gaga, over the moon. "*Mon dieu!* Matching wine to music! Unheard of!" Don explained that this is a process called synesthesia, matching one sensory perception with another, taste and hearing. The French were ecstatic, and so was I.

Because by then, we had planted a bit of Pinot Noir at Sonoma–Cutrer, had fiddled around trying to make Pinot for a few years. We knew that compared with Chardonnay, producing Pinot was a horse of a whole different breed, in more ways than one. Pinot Noir is not Chardonnay, and it's certainly not

179

Cabernet, which is almost impossible to wreck except maybe with a shotgun in the vineyard. Pinot Noir is a whole different thing. It requires artistry. In a documentary movie, *Mondovino (World of Wine)* a French guy says, "To make great Pinot you must have culture." I think it would be a better translation to say "artistry." And here was this guy, Don Blackburn, matching Chardonnay to classical music. Talk about culture. Talk about artistry. Talk about a Renaissance man! I said to myself, "I've gotta get to know this guy, because we're going to make Pinot one of these days, and this is the guy who should do it."

Five years later, when I was ready to make Pinot, I asked Don to come produce it. He declined. "No, I'm very happy here at Bernardus." The following year, I asked him again. He was at a new winery. "No, I'm very loyal to my new owners here." The third year, he was at yet another winery, famous for treating their employees in a certain way, and I said, "Don, what are you doing over there?"

"I'm in charge of the bottling line." Arguably America's finest Pinot Noir winemaker, in charge of the bottling line!

"Well, are you ready to talk now?"

So he came on for our very first vintage, 2004, which (along with several million dollars of other producers' wines), burned up in an arson fire in a warehouse at Mare Island. They got the guy who did it, and he eventually spent some time in the hoosegow, where I hope he gagged on prison-brewed plonk.

So Don made the '04 and '05 and the '06 and '07 and '08. He was the "man" part of our terroir, and he imbued the wine with his spirit. For example, during fermentation, Don was very particular about what kind of music was played. It had to be "Beethoven—but not his early stuff." Can you believe it? Don always got inside every fermentation tank to "press the cap" with his feet, re-submerging the skins daily in the juice as it fermented. In these ways, and many others, he gave the wine his spirit, but the wine was giving him its spirit, too. And, of course, he avoided pumping or filtering the wine. As he explained, "How would you like that kind of treatment done to you?"

When he came in the door to start making Pinot for us, he hadn't been there 10 minutes when he said, "I gotta have my assistant." Of all the winemakers I've ever hired (four), all have said, "I gotta have my assistant." In Don's case, it was good that he did, because after the '08 vintage, we lost Don to spinal cancer, and his assistant, Nicolas Cantacuzene was ready to step right in. He'd already been with Don a few years when they arrived in '04, so he was right there when Don made his '04 through '08 vintages. Nicolas stepped into Don's shoes and carried forth Don's style, or spirit if you will, and the terroir of the wine didn't miss a beat. Nicolas was right there through all five of Don's vintages, so when he stepped up and became the winemaker, he continued with the same soil, same climate, and Don's spirit, or style.

The spirit of Emeritus wine couldn't be more Don Blackburn even today, ten vintages later. I never get through a bottle of our Pinot without a silent prayer of thanks to Don Blackburn.

A bottle of Emeritus Pinot takes Brice on tour of France.
—In Seine Le Good—

CHAPTER FIFTY-TWO

Don's Block and La Combette and Nicolas and David

The month before Don passed, we managed to pick up another piece of land, a hillside five miles away, southwest, a beautiful piece of potential vineyard land. It was a llama farm that I named McDonald Mountain in Don's honor. McDonald was Don, truly a mountain of a man, who hung on long enough to see it so named. In the end, we didn't call it that on the label. We called it Pinot Hill for commercial reasons, but the name of that piece of land is McDonald Mountain.

After we lost Don, Nicolas and I were walking around the Hallberg vineyard, and he said he wanted to make a wine in homage to Don. We went up to one part of the vineyard, and he said, "These four rows will make the wine that Don most strove to achieve, wine with *charm.*"

As Nicolas said, Don always wanted his wine to show charm. One hears this word all the time in Burgundy. There's even a vineyard there called *Les Charmes.* You never hear the word in California or the United States to describe a California wine. Charm. It's just not relevant. We call those four rows "Don's Block." They produce a fabulous, charming wine. According to a French expert, it's just like a Chambolle–Musigny.

At the same time Nicolas chose those vines to produce Don's Block, I said, "While we're at it, let's make a wine in homage to your French heritage." So we trooped all the way across the vineyard, and on a small rise he identified four or five more rows. "These will make the wine that I always hoped to achieve," he said. I agreed. "Okay, in homage to your froggie heritage, we'll rip off a name from your country. There's a vineyard in Burgundy called *Les Combettes,* meaning, 'the little hills.' We'll call this *La Combette* because it's one little hill. And I hope they come after me."

Nicolas was raised in Paris. He enrolled in college there and took his first exam in October. His paper came back all marked up with comments. He went to see *Le Professor*, whose response was, "The appropriate date to talk about this exam, *Nicolah*, is in six months. So, if you wish, *Nicolah*, I'll book you for April 12."

Nicolas packed his bags, got on a plane, flew to California, enrolled at Fresno State University, stayed four years, got his chemistry degree, went to UC Davis, got his masters in enology, and began working with Don Blackburn.

After the 2016 vintage, Nicolas said, "I've been making Pinot most of my life. I'm 50 years old, and I need to get some Chardonnay on my resume. So I took a job with another guy." Two things came instantly to mind: One, Nicolas was 50 years old? How did that happen? I still thought of him as a kid! Two, I needed to find a winemaker.

A very sharp Sonoma wine producer recommended a fellow by the name of David Lattin, who came aboard to produce our '17 vintage. As far as winemaking goes, Dave could be Don Blackburn's twin. Dave's a Burgundian guy. He's been to Burgundy multiple times, worked a harvest there, and he knows the wine people and processes over there. He stepped right into, not Nicolas's, but Don's shoes. In terms of the one-third of terroir that is man, we have been extremely lucky.

And guess what? I think Dave's second vintage with Emeritus, '18, is the best we've ever produced. I couldn't be happier. I've found that a lot of times when business enterprises lose people, the process of replacement ends up being beneficial, and it certainly was this time. But I do like to keep good people. And I pride myself in doing that. That's why we're called Emeritus. Some of the team have been together for over 30 years.

CHAPTER FIFTY-THREE

Fifty Years

Note:

Brice was reluctant to share these words from Tom Eller, president of the Air Force Academy class of 1961, but the fact is, an Academy graduate who never received a star on his shoulder, and didn't die in defense of his country, would seem to be a dark horse at best for this, our first and only class-voted award for the man we consider to be our most outstanding classmate. But you can't begin to know how much care, love, and generosity Brice has shown to our class, our school, our fellow veterans, and anyone who needs a strong shoulder to lean on, a hand to grasp, and the knowledge that there is a good man on our side. I say "our" side because I am one of the beneficiaries of Brice's kindness.

– John Brusky

Having told you this, I give you the class president:

I'm Tom Eller. I was proud to present Brice Jones the 50th Reunion Award at the Class of 1961 Banquet on 4 Nov 2011. 61% of the class voted, and 78% of them voted for Brice Jones to be the recipient of the award.

Brice certainly earned that distinction. He was a decorated combat pilot with the Distinguished Flying Cross, the Bronze

Star, and 14 Air Medals to his credit. He was (and is) a successful businessman, creating the top-rated Chardonnay in America's 3500 Zagat-rated restaurants and number one rated wine
overall for many years. He was inducted into the *Confrérie des
Chevaliers du Tastevin* in Burgundy. He followed up his success-
es by forming a new company, Emeritus Vineyards, with many
of his Sonoma–Cutrer colleagues and employees. To paraphrase
one, Brice's handshake is worth more than a written contract.

He was an active philanthropist, sharing his success with
his classmates, his community, and the less fortunate. In 1985,
Brice's Sonoma–Cutrer Vineyards sponsored an annual charity event that raised money for, among others, the Make-A-
Wish Foundation, the Polly Klass Foundation, and the Magic
Moments Foundation to support children in life-threatening
circumstances. Over the course of years, he grew the event to
achieve net contributions over $1 million/year. At the time of
this award, Brice and Emeritus Vineyards had sponsored five
Hospices of Sonoma charity events to benefit local charities,
Wounded Warriors, and local foster children support organizations.

In 2009, Brice donated two weeks each winter to help
Wounded Warriors learn to ski with their disabilities. In 2010,
he provided financial support to bring an additional 16 Wounded Warriors to the slopes for a week.

Brice was a class leader in developing a strong sense of
unity and esprit de corps as shown by the Class of '61. Brice
directed and partially funded Class Histories for our 25th, 30th,
35th, and 45th Reunions. Brice is a founding member of the
61st Tactical Fighter Squadron (Mythical), a multitude of class-

mates who have gotten together at West Point every two years since 1968 to support USAFA at the biennial Air Force-Army Football Game. Brice helped to establish and endow the annual Roger Stringer Award for Excellence in Inter-Collegiate Debate.

In 1985, Monte Moorberg's remains were repatriated to Travis AFB, CA. Brice arranged for the USAF to fly Monte and his two children to Andrews AFB to be met by an Honor Guard of Classmates.

Brice led the fundraising effort for the Class of 1961, 50th Anniversary Gift to the Academy. The Class responded with a 100% participation rate. This record has not been equaled in the past and will probably never be equaled in the future.

In summary, as a cadet, combat pilot, businessman, and person, Brice has demonstrated our core values of integrity, service, and excellence throughout his life. Brice's numerous and valuable contributions to the International Wine Industry, the US Air Force, the Academy, the Class of 1961, and the Graduate Community, clearly make him first choice for the Class of 1961, 50th Anniversary Outstanding Graduate Award.

CHAPTER FIFTY-FOUR

Chevalier

It's 1999. I'm invited to join the *Confrérie des Chevaliers du Tastevin*, the worldwide ne plus ultra organization of Burgundy lovers. Of course, the Pinot guys over there consider that we make "American" Burgundy over here. But in spite of my wine's place of birth, the "Burgundy Brotherhood" invites me to join. I accept without hesitation.

I figure I'll be "intronized" (inducted) in San Francisco because they have local chapters everywhere. I'll drive down there one night for dinner, and when they call me to the front of the room, they'll hang the *Chevaliers du Tastevin* around my neck. And that will be it. "Oh no," they say, "In your case, we're going to intronize you at World Headquarters. You're coming to the Château du Clos de Vougeot in Burgundy."

After I accept this great honor, somebody tells me that when you're intronized at Clos de Vougeot, you have to give a four-minute acknowledgment to the audience. And my little spiel has to be in French. Oh s**t.

Or should I say, *Merde?*

So I find where there's a French language school near Burgundy. I enroll for two weeks in a full immersion French school, six hours a day, one-on-one with an instructor. Lunch in French, dinner in French—everything in French.

I fly to France two weeks early. One-on-one, six hours a day. At the end of the two weeks, I've got that speech down.

It's the night of the intronization at Clos de Vougeot. The stone chateau is a 16th-century castle, surrounded by vineyards. The Cistercian monks made wine on this site in the 12th century. If the historic ambiance doesn't get you, you've gotta be comatose.

Feeling small but a bit puffed up with pride, and maybe a bit French as well, I'm finally sitting with my sponsors at a table in the great dining hall. The stone walls echo the French chatter of scores of fellow connoisseurs. I smile and act like I understand. They call my name.

I'm the first guy on their list. As I walk to the front of the room, I'm running through the opening lines of my speech. Before you know it, I'm standing facing the Grand Poo-bah, or whatever they call him. I know he's the Grand Poo-bah because his scarlet robes are a little fancier than those of the other poo-bahs. He says some words to me in French, and with great ceremony, he hangs this embossed silver tasting-cup around my neck, the "Tastevin" with a beautiful orange and yellow satin ribbon. Properly festooned, I turn around to begin my speech:

"C'est un grand honneur..."

I feel the Grand Poo-bah's hands on my shoulders. Part of the ceremony, I figure, symbolizing my welcome into the pack. Sort of like the baboon holding up the newborn Lion King so all the animals can genuflect. It's kind of heartwarming, really. But then I realize the guy is simply turning me around. I'm still spieling my memorized speech as he guides me over to the side and says, "Just stand over here."

In other words, *just shut up!*

Well, other people got intronized after me, and they didn't give any speeches either. So my guy in California, who got me to throw away beaucoup francs and spend two weeks of my life with Pierre, *le instructeur de Français,* didn't know his beret from a baseball cap.

But I had it down pat! Two weeks! One-on-one!

At the end of the intronizations, we're having dinner. The Grand Poo-bah comes to my table to say hello...

... and I say,

Brice Cutrer Jones

"C'est un grand honneur..."

CHAPTER FIFTY-FIVE

Mari Jones

I love to ski. Don't know why I didn't mention that earlier, but while my post–Air Force life was unfolding and I was putting down roots in Sonoma County, the call of the slopes kept whispering through the rows of grape vines. So I got help from my brother-in-law, contractor Tom Toedter, and built a small cabin up in the California Sierra near Lake Tahoe, where the kids, Victor, Monte, and Mari all learned to ski. Later, when I sold Sonoma–Cutrer and for a brief period had too much money, I built a really cool, but maybe a bit over-the-top, "cabin" in Telluride, in the Colorado Rockies. I got involved with the Telluride Adaptive Sports Program, sponsoring Wounded Warriors on trips to the area and then skiing with them. And boy! Do they ever have some things to teach us! Attitude, best efforts, graciousness, how to have fun on the slopes. It was and is such a worthy endeavor, I still keep up my sponsorships, which, in a roundabout way, brings us to Mari Cutrer Porth Jones.

My daughter Mari went to Colgate. A year after she graduated, she was considering job options, and I said, "I think I can help land you a job at Telluride Adaptive Sports Program." Well, it didn't take much "influence." They had a slot, and Mari went to work for them. They were so delighted with her they made her director of capital development. She worked there a couple of years and did an outstanding job. Then she got mountain fever and moved off the mountain down to Denver.

I said, "Mari, why don't you come out to Emeritus? We'll find something for you to do here, and you can learn a trade." She came out, and our national sales manager gave her a title, Director of Cellar Door Sales. We didn't really have much of a tasting room, if at all, and we were selling all the wine that we produced, which was a third of our grapes, through our distribution system, selling mainly to restaurants.

Her job would be selling wine out the front door to the people that stopped by. We have a great location right on a main artery, and people would stop by, and she'd sell them wine. Well, this is called direct to consumer, DTC, and it's a huge deal now in the wine business because after the crash of '08, the restaurant business collapsed and never really recovered.

So everybody in our end of the business does DTC, and Mari said, "We need a tasting room." This would've been about five years ago. I said, "Okay, build it."

I got the tasting room consultants in one at a time, took copious notes, and in the end handed them to Mari. She tore them all up and built it her way. We got the contractor in, the architect and so forth, but it was Mari's design, not mine, not the contractor's, not the consultant's, and it is fabulous. The Emeritus tasting room was recently awarded, by a survey in *USA Today*, a position in the top 20 tours of wineries in America. And that position is Number One. (Parental pride showing?)

We owe that all to Mari. What I learned from that is organizations need youth. Youth. Not the old fogeys' way of thinking about tasting rooms and not the consultants' way. Organizations need youth, and I couldn't be happier.

Mari's now in position to assume the mantle of CEO, and everybody's pushing for that. It's not me so much; I'd hold on till my dying breath, like Charlton Heston and his rifle. But everybody else is ready for her to take over, and when that's the case, that's when it succeeds. When everybody else pushes her up, and that's what they're doing, then it succeeds. So I'll soon be auditioning for roving ambassador for Emeritus.

Maybe.

Mari in the vineyard.

Chapter Fifty-Six

Summing Up

Here's what I wrote a year ago, before I passed the baton, before turning 80, before the COVID-19 invasion:

I'm at home in Sausalito, sitting on my balcony, looking out across the bay. Daydreaming. From the horizon beyond the Oakland Bay Bridge, a parade of people advances, growing larger in my mind's eye as they approach, drifting toward me across the water. In front, an 11-year-old boy hitches his pants and begins his dusty 200-mile trek from Perry, Oklahoma to Humboldt, Kansas.

Following my father, my mom, an east-coast Daughter of the Infantry, leads a gaggle of kids, three girls and a boy, military brats from Panama, Texas, Alaska, Virginia, Illinois, California, wherever their society within a society sends them, skipping toward their next relocation, just around the corner. Then come uniformed prep school mischief-makers lobbing tennis balls. Then, Air Force Academy classmates, marching smart and sharp in their parade uniforms, my brothers, always.

Then come:

Monte Larue Moorberg in his g-suit, flight helmet in one hand.

Big George Simler, more concerned about his men than the number of stars on his shoulders.

A continuous succession of guys (women included) who shaped, directed, re-directed, obstructed, and influenced the path of my life.

People saying, "I know a guy who ..."

It dawns on me that the most obvious but easily overlooked aspect of this parade is that often the most important people in my life were those who said no. "No, you can't do that, you've had too much of what you want, you can't fly that plane, you can't go there, you can't grow grapes without irrigation." Dorks behind desks, trying to squeeze me into windowless cubicles.

Here come the Burgundians, who showed me that sometimes man can actually live in harmony with nature and create beautiful things through millenia of trial, error, and lessons learned.

The Americans follow, oblivious of tradition in their brash quest for bigger, better, quicker, but, with their enthusiastic energy, improving upon and advancing the art of guiding a cutting from rooting to cultivation to maturation to harvest, and from there to the glass on your table.

Here comes beautiful, smart, talented, Susan Porth, my eternal love, mother of our three incredible children: Victor, Monte, and Mari. All three of them, thank God, have her spirit in their blood.

All these people, all these roads, all my life.

A freighter plows the choppy water, heading for the Golden Gate and ports unknown.

Ports unknown. The magic of life. The eternal question . . .

"Brice!" a sweet voice from inside the French doors calls.

Oops, got to get ready for dinner. I'm taking Brusk (Remember him?) to Roma's, a fabulous, noisy little joint a few blocks away. I slip a bottle of Hallberg Ranch into the cloth wine caddy I carry to restaurants that tolerate my foibles.

But before we go, I should finish what I started to tell you. I was talking about the eternal question, which is:

"What's the best wine you've ever made?"

Without hesitation, I would answer that with these words:

*"Why, my best wine is the one
I currently have for sale...."*

CHAPTER FIFTY-SEVEN

Weenie Brice

My name is Bill Kosco. I recently discovered that Brice and I shared a common experience as infants. Our fathers were Meteorology grad students at MIT together in 1940. Fourteen years later, in the summer of 1954, my family was transferred to Elmendorf Air Force Base in Anchorage, Alaska. There I met Brice and a lasting friendship began.

Almost immediately, Brice began calling me "Weenie," and if he referred to me when speaking to others, my name was "Weenie Bill." Naturally, he became "Weenie Brice."

It became evident from the beginning that Brice had an aversion to taking no for an answer, any whiff of BS, and playing it safe. That hasn't changed much over the years.

We two weenies shared many experiences. We were on the same Pony League baseball team. We were both Air Explorer scouts and went to Philmont Ranch in New Mexico together. On Kodiak Island's Nebuscan River, we shot the rapids in a leaky boat. And among many adolescent transgressions, we smoked Brice's mother's Camels. I like to think they stunted Brice's growth.

As kids, we could always count on Brice to enliven any situation or event with his "schemes." When school was in session, an Air Force bus took us from the base to Anchorage High. In addition to the teen-aged military "brats" on board, the Air Force provided an AP (Air Policeman) to keep order and provide security. Authority figures always brought out the dark side of Weenie Brice. On more than one occasion, we were reported for disorderly conduct. We would be taken to the AP station, where Colonel Jones was called upon to "bail us out." On one occasion, after a more serious infraction, Brice's dad asked the desk sergeant if he should go home and bring back our toothbrushes. Col. Jones was pretty cool.

In retrospect, it seems clear that Brice applied these early lessons in bucking authority as he progressed (sort of) in his military career.

Upon leaving Alaska, the Jones family was transferred to southern California, and my family went to Pearl Harbor. After high school, Brice accepted an appointment to the Air Force Academy, and I went to the USMA Prep School, entering West Point in 1958. In the winter of '59, we met again after the Army-Air Force game at Yankee Stadium in New York. Brice's Uncle Victor worked in New York (as a male model, believe it or not), and he gave us 30 dollars to go out and celebrate the scoreless tie. Brice had convinced him to bet on the Air Force underdogs, and with the spread of 6 points, Uncle V won some bucks, which he shared with us. Thirty bucks was money enough in those days to have a good time, especially without eighty-dollar bottles of Emeritus on our tab.

I didn't see Weenie Brice again until 1965 in Vietnam. I came in from the field and met him in Saigon. I was immediately impressed by how well he navigated the scene and knew all the establishments and locals. (Don't ask *which* locals or establishments.) Needless to say, his idea of a night out did not include fried rice on the Mekong Floating Restaurant.

Here's another example of our interlaced connections: In October 1969, I married Betty Strauss at West Point. Betty was Bob Strauss's sister. Bob graduated from West Point in 1961. (I was one year behind.) Bob went Air Force and was Brice's classmate at flight school in Big Spring, Texas. They both were given "choice" C-124 assignments. The quotation marks are to denote sarcasm. I really like to needle Weenie Brice about how poorly he and Bob must have performed in flight training in order to merit such an unattractive assignment.

Anyway, after two overseas assignments, Betty and I returned to the States with two daughters, having missed Brice's wedding to Susan Porth. After a year in Newport, RI, we received orders to Schofield Barracks, Hawaii. We took an AMTRAK sleeper to San Francisco, and from there we went to the Larkspur Landing where Brice met us. He was driving a farm vehicle and wearing muddy boots. He was deeply involved at this time, planting his new grape venture. We caught up with current news and met Susan as she was leaving to play softball, but we were able to spend more time with them both when they came to see us in Hawaii.

In the fall of 1984, Brice invited Betty and me to attend the A-AF game at West Point in November. We went but had to redeploy to DC early the next morning after a night of excessive consumption of Sonoma–Cutrer. I was running in the Marine Corps Marathon. It was my last marathon, my body was paying for my bad judgment, and my time was poor. Thanks for the wine, Weenie.

Shortly after that, Brice's group of National Guard and Academy fighter pilot friends grew, and he designated us as the "61st Tactical Fighter Squadron (Mythical)." Under this designation, he would subsequently, through the years, invite us to run the Bay to Breakers, attend his Croquet World Championship Tournaments, spend weekends in Telluride, and, of course, continue the fun at the A-AF games at West Point.

Betty and I were proud to be asked to be Mari's godparents, and we believe it was fate that ordained that Brice's son Monte and our daughter Leigh would graduate from West Point together. Both excelled in their individual sports and had assignments in Iraq.

I have so many warm and wonderful Brice memories, and hopefully, there are more to come.

And now, back to Weenie Brice...

CHAPTER FIFTY-EIGHT

Passing the Baton

It's 2020. Since I finished writing *Pinot Pilot*, a lot has happened. The time had come for me to step back, and I accepted that. Last fall, I couldn't procrastinate any longer, and I passed the baton to Mari. She is now the president of Emeritus, and I am the Emeritus president emeritus, which means, according to my ex-wife, "old guy out to pasture."

As I write this, the country is in lock-down, going through an awful period in its history. Right at the beginning of the COVID-19 crisis, Mari glommed on to what had to be done. Whereas I would have taken weeks to figure I had to do something, she was right on it, and she started immediately cutting management salaries, trimming personnel, furloughing, giving severance in every case. A tough but necessary task. She's doing a great job, and everybody in the company still loves her.

And me? I couldn't be happier. Just as in the rest of my life, when I needed it, along came the right person at the right time.

If I were still at the helm, I'd still be trying to figure out how to tap dance. But Mari did it, and she did it right, and she did it great.

Emeritus will survive, but it will be difficult. Mari's gonna bring in all the rest of the things we need, the right people, the right resources, and we'll get back on track.

I'm so lucky to have Mari. She's going to lead the parade into the future, writing her own story as she marches on, the Emeritus guidon fluttering in the soft Sonoma breeze.

But before I go, I've got one more story to tell you.

CHAPTER FIFTY-NINE

Return to Gooberville

Remember what I said to myself when the judge in the pink bathrobe took my 50 dollars? I told myself that, somehow, I'd get even with him and his town of hijackers.

Well, after two years in Vietnam and a year in Phoenix, I'm assigned to Myrtle Beach, South Carolina. They get fed up with me there and send me down to Fort Walton Beach in Florida—and give me a desk job. I'm a d**k behind a desk! Studying the moon as part of a low-light camera research. The idea was a fighter pilot would have this thing on his wing and bomb a target in low light. Eventually, the conclusion was: "We don't need this piece of crap. Give our pilots half a moon and they can bomb anything." Guess what? The Air Force bought the thing anyway.

So, I'm sitting at my desk in Fort Walton Beach, studying the moon. The phone rings. "Captain Jones, do you know how to fly an F-100?"

"Do I know how to fly an F-100? Hell, yes."

"Come down to the flight line."

Down at the flight line I see the most beautiful F-100 I've ever laid eyes on. It's gleaming, silver—aluminum, not camouflage paint—no tanks, no pods, nothing, sitting there sparkling on the ramp. This is a plane that goes Mach 1 in level flight, and it's just sitting there on the ramp going Mach 1. So beautiful.

"Take this black box, Captain Jones."

It's got dials on top. Turns out to be an element of "Mc-Namara's Fence" across the Ho Chi Minh Trail. They put these boxes down on the trail, and if a truck goes by, it will jiggle and transmit back to somewhere, and they scramble fighters to hit the box, thus, hopefully, hitting a truck or five. So they want to know how far it will transmit.

"Take this box and fly out over the Atlantic as far as you can go until the dials break lock."

"Can do."

"And let us know where it breaks lock."

"Can do."

I put it in my lap, stroke up, take off, get about 20,000 feet above Jacksonville. "Jax Center, I'll be in the local area. I'll let you know when I'm back."

I take it down to tabletop height, under all the radar, get out my little map and put it atop the thing on my lap. I'm screaming up Georgia toward Gooberville, and I see that damned court-house, tallest building in town. I stroke the bird up to 25,000 feet, put the pitot tube on City Hall, and light the burner. Down I plunge, pull out at 3,000 feet and 1.3 Mach. The shock wave has to rattle all the windows on two sides of that building, and—wishful thinking—collapse the roof on the judge's head.

I scream back to Jacksonville, and call those guys waiting for my report. "Hey, guys, I'm 200 miles east of Jacksonville, and it just broke lock."

"Roger. Come back home."

Which I do. With a smile on my face.

The only thing I regret about the whole thing is that I couldn't throw out a note to the judge that said...

"Remember me, you bleep?"

CHAPTER SIXTY

Forget the Pasture

It's Wednesday, September 9, 2020, mid-afternoon. I'm out on my balcony, leaning on the railing, looking out at San Francisco Bay. But I can't see it. Wildfires are burning everywhere. Smoke turns day to night. A menacing orange darkness cloaks the world. Ash floats slowly downward like lazy snowflakes. Two sets of headlights glow as they move slowly along the bayfront street below me. The poisoned air burns my lungs. The bay is a black, gloomy and silent abyss. No brass bands and parades march towards my balcony through the sunlit mists of my memories.

No cheerful female voice calls from within the house, reminding me that we're going out for dinner. I'm all alone. Just me, the smoke, the gloom, and my thoughts.

The vineyards are safe but extensive smoke has ruined the crop. We're trying to deal with a few tons of grapes here and there, but mostly it's a total loss. COVID-19 and the fires are teaming up on me.

A foghorn moans across the dark water.

I snap out of it.

What's the matter with me? I can still fly! No more "President Emeritus." No more "old guy out to pasture." I grab my car keys and head for the door. Got things to do!

In the car, I resist putting it in afterburner. Heading up to the winery now at a slow and steady 80 mph.

We'll be back.
The sun will be back.
The grapes will come back.

I'll be back. Better than ever.

Like my fighter pilot friend said:
"You can't hang Brice Jones."

Afterwords

THANKS TO THE FOLLOWING
FOR THEIR VIEWPOINTS, OPINIONS,
AND REMEMBRANCES.

SAM HARDAGE – Classmate, mentor

"Brice says it took him 35 years to break the code on how to make world-class vino, but unless you have the curiosity and the drive, you can spend all those years gaining 'experience,' but nothing will have changed."

WEENIE BILL KOSCO - Many-Motors pilot, life-long weenie

"Brice had an aversion to taking no for an answer, any whiff of BS, and playing it safe."

TOM ELLER - President, USAFA Class of 1961

*"Brice's handshake is worth
more than a written contract."*

GERRY DAWES- Swabbie, gourmet, adoring fan

*"First, you hold your glass up to
the light to see the color. Now
you see this classic color that we
call in Spanish orina de caballo,
or horse p—."*

CHUCK BENNETT- Business cohort, marketing guru

*"People worked for him and went to the
mat for him and broke their backs for
him because of that kind of feeling of
inspiration that great generals bring
to the table, not because he was such a
brilliant, bureaucratic-style manager of
people, you know?*

MICHAEL LAVENSON- National Sales Director, Emeritus Vineyards

"There were two rock stars in California wine. Brice was Mick Jagger. Robert Mondavi was more like John Lemmon. Brice was more 'The Bad Guy.' I remember him selling Sonoma–Cutrer to Brown-Forman at landmark prices then telling them to go (bleep) off."

HECTOR NEGRONI - Classmate, role model

"When he was still in the Air Force and trying his best to get out, he started wearing a red tie with his uniform and letting his hair grow long."

JIM HINKLE- Classmate, pilot, business cohort

"They played taps and lowered the flag. That was our signal to run up the hill and take Brice prisoner."

Sisterwords

This is family stuff, nothing to do with wine, but when your sisters tell you they have something to say, you gotta sit back, keep your mouth shut, put on a helmet, and look out.

SISTER MARILYN - Contrarian

"Brice called, 'Hey, Marilyn, come over here. We have a fun game.' And, sucker that I was, I went over there."

SISTER EMILIA - Possessor of nine toes

"And now, presenting Brice the Magnificent."

SISTER ELEANOR - Now known as "Fithian"

"Happily, it was through that shattering experience that his humanity, his natural generosity and empathetic nature, came to the fore."

Sister Marilyn:

I told you how Brice treated me when I was four years old, bouncing my head down the stairs, how Mom's attempts at making him a *perfect little gentleman* were futile. And what do I get for my honesty? Shoved back here to the end of the book, and—one more petty slight from my big brother—*he italicizes me!* Well, truth will out. Here's another childhood memory:

Mom was trying to prep me for my first visit to the dentist, a military dentist and—well, you don't even want to know about them. So, Mom was trying to calm me, and Brice cuts in with a taunting voice: "Oh, so you're going to the dentist? The dentist!" And Mom says, "Now Brice, go into the other room." And Brice says, "No, they take a needle, Marilyn, and it's *this long,* and it has waves in it, and they put it in your mouth, and it goes right through your cheek!" So Mom took me to the car screaming and crying for my very first dentist visit.

Here's another one:

I have a lifelong fear of being in close places, because, again in Arlington, when I was maybe 7 and walking home, there was this big vacant lot, and Brice was there with a couple of his friends. I think he was 11 or 12 years old. And in the vacant lot there was a big refrigerator carton lying on its side, and Brice called, "Hey, Marilyn, come over here. We have a fun game." And, sucker that I was, I went over there.

"Get in the box, and if you knock three times, we'll let you out."

"You will not!" I whined.

"Sure, we will. Watch!" One of the kids gets in the box, knocks three times, they let him out. "OK, get in there." They lock me in, and off they go.

Knocked three times. Knocked three hundred times. Knocked three thousand times! Now I'm crying. I have no idea how long I was in there. Then here comes my sister Eleanor walking along with two of her friends, and she sees the refrigerator box shaking, and hears someone inside screaming. Over they come, open the box.

"Sister!" I scream. "Oh, Brice wouldn't let me out!"

To this day, I have claustrophobia.

Sister Emilia:

I was the youngest, so he called me Baby all the time, until I was old enough to tell him to stop.

One of my early memories of Brice: I was 3 years old, and we were living in Arlington. It was summer, and I was out playing with my sisters. I was riding on the back of my 11-year-old sister's bicycle in my bare feet. And the next thing I knew, I looked down, and there was my big toe on the ground. The bicycle spokes had just taken it right off.

Brice had the incredible presence of mind to pick me up, talk soothingly to me, and just very calmly carry me home. And my poor mom, she let out a whoop, and that set me off. She got me right in the car to drive me to the dispensary, and I will always remember Brice sitting in the back seat—he was so calm and quick-thinking. He had his little Boy Scout training, so he ripped up his shirt into strips and wrapped it around my foot. You know, to keep me from bleeding to death, I guess. He was just 13.

The fact that I can still, all these years later, look down and see where my big toe ought to be is probably why such an early childhood memory is so indelibly imprinted in my brain.

Another memory I have of Brice is when we were snowed in at our cabin in Alaska. I was 5 then, and Brice would have been 15.

Evidently, we were running low on food, and we couldn't get out. And I guess a decision was made that my dad would stay back with us to watch over his family, and Brice volunteered to walk out with his friend. I remember asking where

Brice was, and they told me he was out delivering his papers, on his paper route.

The next thing I remember is that we were all standing out in front of the cabin, and there's this big military helicopter landing, snow is blowing, the helicopter door opens, and there's Brice smiling and waving at us.

You can see how I grew up with this larger than life idea about Brice. Just comes swooping in. And, of course, he had left home by the time I was about seven. He went off to the Academy, so it was, you know, years of swooping in at Christmas and just impressing us all to pieces. I think it's really only when we all became adults and got married, had kids, had adult lives that we got to know each other in a different way.

But that's how I remember Brice: always coming to the rescue. He was like my favorite uncle. I remember my birthday parties in Alaska. We had them in the basement, and Brice would put on a magic show, and he made this little stage with sheets for curtains, and his friend Bill Kosco's voice coming from behind the curtains: "And now, presenting Brice the Magnificent!" And the sheets would open and there he was with his magic tricks.

I thought that was the coolest thing in the world.

Sister Fithian:

O ur brother Brice was our parents' only son. So, growing up he was hovered over and pampered. It was only after the experience of war combat was he enabled to find a way to express what had always been latent: He became a thoughtful son, brother, and friend, who, through that trauma, had found a means to express himself emotionally and empathetically. On his return from war, he would often weep at the tragedy of others, sometimes even strangers.

In the late forties when Brice and I were still quite young, our family lived for a short time on an Air Force base near Rapid City, SD. He must have been maybe seven and I was five. The only kids around were from a nearby Indian reservation. Nearly every morning we would all gather on the edge of the base and start running in one direction, then, after a couple hours, turn around and run back to the base. This went on for weeks at a time. As a five year old, I could barely keep up. But I did, and that's what still stands out in my memory. Maybe, for all I know, Brice was right behind me.

Some years later, when we lived in Arlington, VA, Brice had a newspaper route. One Christmas morning, Dad took Brice out in the Plymouth station wagon to deliver his papers. I got to go along. It is a happy memory, of me actually helping my big brother do something. It was a good feeling.

As a boy, Brice had been poured into a soldier's life by his legacy of two generations of military men. It seems to me, he was only able to access his emotional life much later as a young man, after experiencing the trauma of war combat. Happily, it was through that shattering experience that his humanity, his natural generosity and empathetic nature, came to the fore. As a result, he matured into a self-aware and deeply feeling person.

Brice demonstrates his humanity through his very evident love for his family of origin as well as the generations growing up around him. He has taken seriously the self-described role of "head of family" in the best sense of that moniker...where he pays attention to the care of his family. That same sense of caring extends into his long-standing friendships with his Air Force buddies. As a result, he is looked upon with affection and loving tolerance for a famous (or infamous?) Cutrer Jones family trait: our singular and individual eccentricities. Each of us siblings is, as our mother used to say, "very unique." Yep, we sure are. And we show our love for each other all the time, despite or because of, our "unique" traits.

The "very unique" Jones kids. In descending height:
Brice, Eleanor (now known as Fithian), Marilyn, Emilia

THE END
of the beginning